Perspectives on Higher Education: Impact of the COVID-19 Pandemic

EDITED BY
PROFESSOR ABDULRAHMAN O AL-YOUBI
PROFESSOR ABDULMONEM AL-HAYANI
PROFESSOR JUDY MCKIMM

Edited by

Professor Abdulrahman O Al-Youbi
University President
Chemistry Department, Faculty of Science,
King Abdulaziz University, Jeddah, Saudi Arabia

Professor Abdulmonem Al-Hayani
University Vice President for Educational Affairs
Department of Anatomy, Faculty of Medicine,
King Abdulaziz University, Jeddah, Saudi Arabia

Professor Judy McKimm
Professor of Medical Education and Director of Educational Strategic
Development, Swansea University Medical School, Swansea University,
Wales, UK

ISBN: 979 8 67 266908 3
First published 2020.

Contents

Contributors

Prof Abdulrahman O Al-Youbi
University President
Chemistry Department, Faculty of Science
King Abdulaziz University, Jeddah, Saudi Arabia

Prof Abdulmonem Al-Hayani
University Vice President for Educational Affairs
Department of Anatomy, Faculty of Medicine
King Abdulaziz University, Jeddah, Saudi Arabia

Prof Sherif Elsaadany
Professor of Infectious Diseases
King Abdulaziz University, Saudi Arabia &
Tropical Medicine and Infectious Diseases Department, Faculty of Medicine
Tanta University, Egypt

Prof Ayman Elsamanoudy
Professor of Clinical Biochemistry, Faculty of Medicine
King Abdulaziz University, Jeddah, Saudi Arabia &
Medical Biochemistry and Molecular Biology, Faculty of Medicine
Mansoura University, Mansoura, Egypt

Dr Mohammed Hassanien
Associate Professor, Medical Education and Clinical Biochemistry
King Abdulaziz University, Jeddah, Saudi Arabia &
Medical Biochemistry Department, College of Medicine
Tanta University, Tanta, Egypt

Associate Prof Paul Jones
Programme Director, Graduate Entry Medical Programme, Swansea University Medical School, Swansea University, Wales, UK

Prof Judy McKimm
Professor of Medical Education and Director of Educational Strategic
Development
Swansea University Medical School, Swansea University, Wales, UK

Chloe Mills
Independent consultant and English editor
PhD candidate, Swansea University, Wales, UK

Dr Sameh Salah Youssef
Associate Professor of Translation
English Department, College of Science and Arts
King Abdulaziz University, Jeddah, Saudi Arabia

Foreword

We are proud to introduce this book *Perspectives on Higher Education: Impact of the COVID-19 Pandemic*, which is the first in a series of books produced by King Abdulaziz University tackling current global issues in higher education.

Designed to provide different viewpoints on contemporary topics in higher education from an international perspective, this first book aims to provide a reference for those interested in higher education worldwide, as it explores mechanisms of actions taken during crises, with a special focus on the COVID-19 pandemic. It is a quick guide for those working and learning in universities around the globe facing the impacts and consequences of COVID-19. The book brings together the major strands of topics relevant to higher education, such as learning, teaching, assessment, and research. It aims to help readers acquire an understanding of how the higher education system might function under stress, sketching a conceptual map for the interested reader. The aim of this book is not to present a unified approach to deal with distressing situations in higher education, as different contexts dictate different solutions, nor to promote any single current approach. Rather, it aims to explore a wider range of perspectives from around the world in all their richness and variety so that the reader may gain ideas on a range of topics.

We believe that by sharing common issues, strategies and solutions, we can help alleviate some of the impacts of the pandemic on university systems and on administrators, faculty, staff, and students. Further, we believe that every problem contains a solution and, in the middle of difficulty, opportunity lies. Therefore, most of the topics discussed address everyday life and issues in universities: learning, teaching and assessment, research, faculty and learner wellbeing, leadership and change. The book concludes with a look forward into what will probably be new ways of working and learning.

Exploring the impact of COVID-19 on higher education is a very broad and diverse topic, and therefore keeping the book to a manageable size involved a firm selection process of topics. Inevitably, the selection of topics is not fully comprehensive, but this book is a step on a long road to explore the effects of crisis situations on higher education. We hope that readers will gain a feel for what the impact of a pandemic on higher education is like, and that the book stimulates interest in exploring these and other issues further.

The book is organized in chapters, with each chapter being independent, comprising an introduction and overview of a topic. However, the chapters collectively integrate to provide a broader overview of the multiple complex issues that have recently arisen, and may give insights on how to deal with similar situations in the future. The book brings together various concepts and ideas on key areas of university life from the perspectives of various stakeholders, linked to real-life examples and supported by relevant literature and a broad spectrum of case studies. The book also opens the door for scholars to investigate and explore additional aspects of the topic.

We have enjoyed putting the book together, and we hope that readers around the globe enjoy reading it and find it useful in different contexts. Last, but not least, we hope that this book will add another dimension to how people think about the impact of pandemics and other crisis situations on higher education.

Professor Abdulrahman O Al-Youbi
University President
Chemistry Department, Faculty of Science,
King Abdulaziz University, Jeddah, Saudi Arabia

Professor Abdulmonem Al-Hayani
University Vice President for Educational Affairs
Department of Anatomy, Faculty of Medicine,
King Abdulaziz University. Jeddah Saudi Arabia

Acknowledgements

First and foremost, we write this book with great respect for the hundreds of thousands of people who have lost their lives to this virus, or who have made great sacrifices to support those affected by COVID-19. We thank health, care and essential support workers worldwide for their heroic actions. We would like to acknowledge the support from King Abdulaziz University and the contributions of all the authors and the case studies provided by colleagues around the world. As ever, we also acknowledge the part played by the students and faculty in our universities from whom we continue to learn so much.

A special thank you is given to the following additional contributors to the book:

Dr. Abdulrahman Alkhorayef, Ministry of Education and Al-Imam Mohammad Ibn Saud Islamic University, Riyadh, Saudi Arabia
Prof. Abdulrahman H. Altalhi, King Abdulaziz University, Jeddah, Saudi Arabia
Dr. Abid A. Almashaikhi, King Abdulaziz University, Jeddah Saudi Arabia
Prof. Adel Abuzenadah, King Abdulaziz University, Jeddah, Saudi Arabia
Prof. Hana Abdullah Al-Nuaim, University Vice President of Women's Campus, King Abdulaziz University, Jeddah, Saudi Arabia
Dr. Hani Brdesee, King Abdulaziz University, Jeddah, Saudi Arabia
Dr. Hani Choudhry, King Abdulaziz University, Jeddah, Saudi Arabia
Dr. Hisham Bardesi, King Abdulaziz University, Jeddah, Saudi Arabia
Dr. Naif Al-Johani. King Abdulaziz University, Jeddah, Saudi Arabia
Prof. Saud M. Alsulami, King Abdulaziz University, Jeddah, Saudi Arabia
Prof. Tawfeek A. Al-khyal, King Abdulaziz University, Jeddah, Saudi Arabia
Prof. Yusuf A. Al-Turki, King Abdulaziz University, Jeddah, Saudi Arabia
Reem Almutairi, final stage PhD candidate, Swansea University, UK
Dale Firth, 3rd year undergraduate Physics student, Swansea University, UK

Chapter 1

An Overview of the Impact of the Pandemic on Universities

Professor Judy McKimm
Professor Sherif Elsaanady

Across the globe, university leaders, administrators, teachers and their learners (at all stages of education and training) are making rapid adaptations to their educational provision and other activities as a consequence of the COVID-19 pandemic, whilst living in severe uncertainty. This is affecting all levels of education, from undergraduate and postgraduate education, to doctoral and research supervision and faculty development, as well as research and administrative activities. Alongside this, there has been huge social disruption with many countries experiencing various levels and stages of lockdown and social distancing arrangements.

In this introduction we summarise the challenges, strategies and opportunities for higher education that have arisen as a consequence of the pandemic, presenting both a Saudi Arabian and an international perspective. This book represents students and educators, and draws on a number of models such as the COINNS framework, a simple, practical, creative yet action-oriented framework (McKimm, 2009). COINNS is formed from the stages that are considered as individuals or groups work through the model: Challenges, Opportunities, Ideas, Needs and Next Steps.

In terms of the higher education response to COVID-19, Box 1.1 sets out some questions (which can apply at any level, university, department, programme, course/module) to help us move forward. In this chapter we will take some of these questions and provide some initial ideas and strategies that will be further developed and expanded throughout the book.

Aside from the social disruption arising from the pandemic, the educational **challenges**, problems or issues that need to be considered include: maintaining the continuity of the education and training provision itself; facilitating continuation of research and supervision; planning and implementing recruitment and selection processes for the next cohorts of learners; and managing assessment, progression and graduation in a fair and equitable way, whilst maintaining academic standards.

Universities are also responsible for the physical and psychological safety and wellbeing of their learners and faculty, which, at an individual level may well involve helping and supporting people to cope with change and uncertainty, such as allaying student and faculty fears, supporting them to change behaviours to work effectively from home, or looking after and supporting students who are isolated away from home, or who have returned home and are now at a distance from university. This might mean universities are unable to completely close, but need to maintain support and other essential services.

The context in which a university operates has to be considered first, as government and local guidance must be incorporated into actions and advice. This pandemic will occur in waves around the world, and so, when re-occupation of buildings and campuses is being considered, physical safety is paramount and maintaining social distancing for staff and students is a huge challenge. Universities will need to choose how to phase-in returns to campus, whether by programme, department, building or by requiring all those who can work and study easily at home to continue doing so.

Airlines around the world have suffered due to the COVID-19 pandemic, as nations worldwide closed their borders in an attempt to contain the pandemic (Salcedo et al., 2020). Universities have advised their staff to suspend any activity that may require them to travel abroad, until there is a return to normalcy. What adds to the challenges is that many faculty members have already made arrangements through paying for tickets and conference registration fees from university funds. Many universities worldwide have asked international students not to travel and instead continue their studies from home, as they may be at risk of infection. These travel restrictions naturally impact the flexible, international nature of universities across the world.

Maintaining effective and timely communications when faculty are working remotely and students have returned home is a major challenge, particularly in terms of the wider organisation, its leadership and management. Managing uncertainty in a daily-changing external environment requires developing effective and frequent communication routes among teachers and learners. Robust digital services are central when face-to-face communication cannot happen and leaders need to continually ask themselves:

> *What information needs to be communicated?*
> *Who needs to be informed and when?*
> *How can we best communicate – what medium should we use?*
> *How can we keep in touch with people as things change?*

Whilst some of these challenges will be experienced by all stakeholders, other challenges will be more context- or role-dependent. As many countries are shifting to remote digital management systems, home working and online learning, a robust technological infrastructure becomes even more essential. Some of the issues that universities, their faculty and their learners (and not just in low resource settings) have had to address include remote access to university systems (e.g. quality assurance, student record, finance and assessment management systems) from home, non-availability of devices (e.g. laptops) to lower socioeconomic groups of students and teachers, and difficulties with network bandwidths and connections.

Another useful model which can help university leaders formulate strategy is the 'Whole brain' perspective (Herrmann & Herrmann-Nehdi, 2015) which requires a purposeful use of all four quadrants of our brains, considering the following (in this order):

Economic risks for universities

Universities are educational institutions, where faculty teach and conduct research while undergraduate and postgraduate students learn, and they are key employers and a driving force of economy both locally and regionally (Illanes, 2020). Because universities serve such a wide variety of functions, coping with COVID-19 has been particularly complicated. Several universities also operate hospitals which serve as buffer zones for the healthcare system. The number of university stakeholders is therefore huge, and university revenue models are complicated, comprising revenues from tuition, endowments, donations, and research grants.

As the pandemic forces many students to return home, it has affected the budgets of universities dependent on considerable tuition fees and costs of accommodation and living (Alston, 2020). If the slowdown continues, this may have devastating consequences on public higher education budgets, and therefore universities may face budget cuts in the next year or two. Many universities may be less prepared today to help students through the pandemic, and this could be the difference between tudents being able to pursue their studies or having to abandon their educational dreams (Roubein et al., 2020).

Students may leave their campus, but they cannot ignore COVID-19. Illanes (2020) states that employees are concerned about their careers, research projects are on hold, and admissions are unclear. Meanwhile, students may have pressing unanswered queries on (amongst others) determining academic credits, reimbursements, effects on athletic scholarships or residency issues in case a student visa is cancelled.

In the wake of the novel coronavirus pandemic, failure to transition to online education may force some universities to be at risk of permanent closure (Bothwell, 2020b), although other, more adaptive higher education or commercial organisations may gain financially. Increasing numbers of American, European and Asian universities have closed their campuses and switched to online classes as they begin preparing for closures that might run for several months or even longer.

The pandemic has caused immediate, medium and long-term employment risks for casual employees in occupations with high exposure to the public. Ross (2020) suggests that the coronavirus crisis will aggravate the already precarious financial situation of many students, and this damage may last for many years. Risks include students on part-time jobs where they may have an elevated likelihood of catching the disease because they are in regular contact with people. Although the danger the virus poses to the young appears relatively low, infection means a period without wages. Whether or not students get sick, they are among the most likely in the community to suffer financial hardships. Students working full-time jobs also face problems of layoff as casual staff members are *always the first to go"*. As international students are ineligible for income support, and most of them have no family in the country of study, their situation is of a particular concern.

However, we have also seen many students and universities rise to the challenge of engaging with local, regional and international collaborations. The case studies in this chapter set out some of the activities undertaken by students at King Abdulaziz and Swansea Universities to help their local communities.

BOX 1.3   CASE STUDY: SOCIAL ACCOUNTABILITY OF KAU STUDENTS DURING THE COVID-19 PANDEMIC

No sooner had the COVID-19 pandemic emerged than the urgent need for community solidarity and community-based initiatives became more pressing. There were numerous initiatives to support the most vulnerable community sectors suffering from COVID-19 effects. KAU students were at the heart of all this as they launched several initiatives during the pandemic. Community initiatives of KAU students included participation with King Abdulaziz Medical Center to deliver medicines for patients with long-term conditions, especially the elderly, and for those who were unable to access the Medical Center due to the lockdown or for fear of infection. KAU students also developed several awareness initiatives to limit the spread of coronavirus. These initiatives included developing a number of awareness videos, paper and electronic brochures on precautionary measures for protection from the virus.

Furthermore, students of health colleges and University scouts developed a number of voluntary initiatives as they organized awareness campaigns in commercial markets and malls, conducting some simple medical checkups for the clients of these markets, and orienting them with COVID-19 precautionary measures and prevention methods. Moreover, a number of Faculty of Pharmacy students, after intensive training courses, volunteered to work in the King Abdulaziz University Pharmacy to help the pharmacy staff.

Learning and Teaching

Decisions will need to be made around maintaining learning and teaching continuity and these are discussed in detail in Chapter 2. Briefly, decisions will need to be kept under continual review as the pandemic takes its course and some decisions will be made at programme level, including consideration of moving start or graduation dates for programmes or deciding how much (if any) to change a programme. The main strategy and challenge for universities worldwide is to shift to online distance learning.

Initially, universities will have to determine what technologies are already in place and whether they need to invest in new technologies, depending on the number of people needing to use the system, what functionality is required and cyber-security needs. Whilst web-based platforms can easily be used for meetings and webinar type activities, for learning and teaching the system might need to host video streaming or have the capacity to store large sets of resources. Obviously some platforms are better than others for mass education and, if a platform already exists, then this needs to be assessed to ensure it can cope with the shift to online learning and communications. Then, staff and student training and support are needed to ensure that teachers and students know how to use the systems effectively.

In terms of learning technologies, a wide range of technologies exist that can be used to enhance teaching and learning. But any tool chosen must be for educational reasons, not simply because it is available. As with any learning event, starting with what you are trying to achieve (the learning outcomes) comes first; then, you can move onto how it can best be achieved, because there are both advantages and disadvantages to using technology in teaching and learning.

Across the globe, teachers in all sectors are having to become familiar with a range of different platforms available for teaching and learning that they may have not used before, and learners and faculty are both experiencing technology-related challenges, many of which have been reported previously (Muilenburg & Berge, 2005). Some are connectivity-related e.g. internet bandwidth or infrastructure, whereas others are device-related, e.g. incompatible software or lack of access. In fact, one barrier to online learning is access to the required technology, with many learners facing challenges due to lack of internet or computer access.

These issues may be related to economic status and thus access to technology is an issue that must be addressed sensitively. Due to connectivity/access problems, learners and teachers might turn to using smart phones more than tablets or computers, but these devices are more limited in functionality with many apps either being unavailable or not having all the features of the campus-based version. Furthermore, the IT support provided by institutions varies widely. Thus, universities need to make sure that all learners and especially those who have limited access to technology are not incurring high costs associated with the use of technology, such as mobile data, particularly if videos or other resources that require streaming are used. As learners and teachers make the shift to online learning, it is essential that the organisational infrastructure fully supports online learning and provides additional faculty development to train the trainers for new ways of teaching and support learners in new ways of learning and engagement. The support offered by IT must be comprehensive, non-judgmental, and fair. Above all else, educators must attempt to remove the barriers to online learning and ensure a level playing field for all. Universities must understand the unique circumstances of all learners and remember that online learning is not "one size fits all", but is a process that must be continually adjusted.

BOX 1.4   CASE STUDY: STUDENTS STEPPING UP TO SUPPORT LOCAL COMMUNITIES

The strain on UK health workers during the COVID-19 crisis was immense and was exacerbated by most schools not being open which meant that workers with children of school age were often unable to work. A group of medical students in Swansea University identified this as a major issue and set up a childcare service which helped not only health workers and healthcare lecturers in universities, by providing a safe environment for the children to be cared for by individuals who were already in the health profession (as students) and who had been checked in relation to child protection issues. The service was extremely successful and served to allow health care workers to return to their clinical duties without unduly worrying about who was looking after their children. Other healthcare professionals from around the country also learned from this and also set up similar services in their own communities, benefitting many hundreds of workers.

Educators face specific challenges in adapting their teaching to online and distance formats. The rapidity of the shift to online learning and teaching due to the pandemic has been a problem, particularly when staff might also be working from home with many other demands on their time without access to their usual resources and support. Conducting online teaching and virtual meetings can be tiring as a lot of concentration on computer screens and other devices is required, and those with other duties such as clinical work or family responsibilities may feel overloaded. Many faculty lack confidence and competence in providing online learning, both technologically and pedagogically, and even those experienced with online education can feel they are adapting learning and teaching activities *"on the fly"*, with insufficient time to prepare and develop high quality learning activities. Teachers with international students, who have returned home because of the COVID-19 crisis, may find it difficult to organize synchronous online sessions suitable for all time zones. Aside from the pedagogical aspects, which need to focus on facilitating learning, achieving a practical balance between synchronous (real time) and asynchronous (learners engaging in their own time) learning will depend on a number of factors, including the geographical location of the students, the number of the students, the educator's availability and the programme.

The main challenges educators may experience relating to learners will be around maintaining motivation and nurturing continued engagement with learning activities from a distance when programmes and learners' lives have been completely disrupted. In live teaching sessions, additional issues may be encountered related to ensuring in-class engagement and interactions. Educators may well find themselves working hard to encourage participants to adapt to new teaching and learning methods in a number of ways, and must acknowledge cultural and interpersonal sensitivities and preferences when implementing policies, such as turning on video and audio in online sessions. Finally, judging the effectiveness of learning during disruption and change may be difficult and the usual quality assurance and feedback mechanisms may have to be adapted.

BOX 1.5   CASE STUDY: MEDICAL STUDENTS BECOMING PART OF THE HEALTH WORKFORCE

Many medical schools around the world were left with difficult decisions to make as their final year students had not taken their final examinations before the COVID-19 crisis struck. Swansea University Medical School final year medical students were in the fortunate position to have completed all their knowledge-based and clinical examinations before the end of December and so many had already passed the requirements to graduate. The UK National Health Service (NHS) was keen for as many final year medical students as possible to qualify early (before the usual time in August) so that they could become part of the NHS workforce to help with the crisis and the workforce sickness levels at that time. The process of allowing them to qualify early took time to organise as liaison had to be carefully carried out between the University, the General Medical Council (GMC) and the UK Government.

In the interim, many of the students worked helping in both primary and secondary care as healthcare support workers until their early registration with the GMC came through. The vast majority of final year medical students from Swansea (as with most other UK medical schools) qualified early and were working in the NHS before the August crossover of doctors in training. This has had a number of benefits, including providing a better preparation for working as a junior doctor as they were often working alongside other doctors in training. Finally, there will be a smoother handover in August than usual, as the new doctors will have been working for a few months in their roles and will be more familiar with the practices in their respective hospitals.

For all programmes, knowledge-based activities are more straightforward to provide and 'convert' to an online format than those which require face-to-face contact, practical activities and specialised equipment in laboratories, fieldwork, studio work, simulation or professional placements. For professional programmes (such as health, medicine, law or social work) the inability to provide industry or clinical placements (whether in-country or overseas) may require some very deft footwork to redesign programmes. Whilst some simulated activities (such as virtual laboratories or virtual patients) may assist in enabling students to achieve their learning outcomes, they will probably be insufficient to allow achievement of specific skill or competencies. These issues are of specific importance for final year students nearing graduation who may need to graduate to enter a professional register.

Assessment and Progression

Assessment planning and delivery will be a major challenge at all stages, both for knowledge-based assessment as well as practical or professional assessment, particularly in relation to senior students nearing graduation. Programmes that rely heavily on a final end-of-year or end-of-programme assessment will be particularly vulnerable if these are not able to be undertaken safely in a face-to-face context. For those responsible for programmes, depending on when the pandemic strikes and the responses by governments, fundamental questions need to be asked about the purpose and nature of planned assessments, in terms of why and what are we assessing, when and how are we assessing and if we change assessment mode or format, what unintentional consequences might there be?

Whilst progression for final year students needs to be a priority so that they can graduate, for students in the earlier years of a degree, it may be possible to calculate a grade from course work or previous examinations to enable them to progress to their next year of study. Students who are struggling academically may have been relying on boosting their grades in a final examination and they may therefore be adversely affected. It may be deemed that not all the planned assessments are essential, or that assessments may be able to be deferred until students return to campus, even if this is a subsequent year. If assessments are essential and they have to be run online, then this raises additional issues both in terms of practicalities of running the assessments, ensuring access to the assessment is fair and equitable (with regard to time zones, devices, a quiet space, web access and bandwidth) as well as ensuring that students are behaving with integrity and not cheating. See Chapter 3 for information on assessments.

Research and Supervision

Research activities are also affected, both for academics and learners. The main question to ask (and this will vary immensely) is can an individual's or group's research continue if campuses are closed and facilities needed (such as laboratories, equipment or access to research participants) are unavailable. Universities need to prioritise their research activities based on a number of factors. For universities with strong biosciences research, many laboratories may be well-placed to carry out research directly relating to the pandemic, in terms of vaccine development or treatments. Other research groups may be able to refocus on social or behavioural, economic or modelling activities. Other research activities may be deemed crucial to the university's endeavours, although these will need to be managed in line with physical distancing and safety guidance. Additional equipment such as PPE (personal protective equipment) or screens may therefore need to be purchased.

For students, many of the above issues will also need to be addressed, but their ability to continue research activities will also depend on their stage of postgraduate education and where they are located, as many students may well return to their homes. Students at a very early stage when they are still developing their research questions and doing their literature review, or those at the writing up stage, may well be able to continue their studies as long as they have access to online resources including library access. For students at the data gathering stage, this may be much more problematic, depending on the government guidance and situation. For example, if the research requires access to specialised equipment or face-to-face access to certain contexts such as schools (which may be closed), or certain groups of study participants, then the student may have no option but to put their research on hold until the situation changes.

In some cases, the research may be able to be modified, for example carrying out telephone or video interviews, but in many cases this will not be possible. This then raises issues regarding progression requirements which will need to be addressed. Students may have to be advised to suspend studies or be awarded an extension to studies, but for students on scholarships or bursaries this may be problematic. Supervision can be carried out remotely fairly effectively as can assessment vivas or oral examinations, however, for the latter the experience for the student is not the same as a face-to-face viva and might raise equality issues. For further information on research and supervision in the pandemic, see Chapter 5.

Longer Term and Wider Considerations

For the international university sector, the pandemic has been a great blow, with huge costs related to additional spending on systems, equipment, training and development and administrative support, compounded by the potential loss of income from research grants and other activities (accommodation, conferencing and consultancy) and potentially lower numbers of students, especially international students, in the coming academic year.

Depending on the decisions of governments in regard to school systems, national examinations may be affected and, if university campuses are closed, interviews and face-to-face selection methods may not be possible. This poses issues for the recruitment and selection of students for the next academic year. On what do we base our decisions on offering students a place, when the usual metrics are unavailable or possibly unreliable? How do we design the actual selection process itself? How will we compensate for face-to-face selection methods? The wider context is also uncertain because it is virtually impossible to predict how the pandemic will elapse throughout our increasingly interconnected world, what restrictions there will be on travel, and what the economic global impact will be, on specific countries and regions, on universities themselves, and on individuals.

In some countries, students are demanding reimbursement for accommodation costs because they have had to return home to their families, and some are seeking fee reimbursement because they feel the online provision that has been put together was not adequate or not what they signed up for. These issues can affect the reputation of the university and those which have responded slowly or less than adequately have been most affected. So, maintaining quality assurance systems and *"taking the temperature"* of how the shifts in provision are impacting all stakeholders is essential. A more detailed look forward is described in Chapter 7.

Conclusions

This chapter has outlined some of the key challenges and issues that need to be addressed by universities and individuals as a result of the COVID-19 pandemic. In summary, the lessons that have already being learned by educators are:

- *Safety is paramount, communication and transparency is key*
- *Flexibility is needed from all stakeholders*
- *Technologies can help, but be realistic*
- *Acknowledge the need for psychological adaptation to change and crisis*
- *Tap into the wisdom and collegiality of the community*

(McKimm, Bishop, Jones and Gibbs, 2020)

Whilst it is vital in this 'crisis' stage to maintain the continuity of university life as much as possible, universities must also keep an eye on the future and the changes that should be made downstream, whatever the future may hold.

We should ask ourselves what we should stop doing (the *"expendable"*), what might we start doing (the *"new"*) and what should we continue (the *"precious"*), in order to enable staff and students to work and learn effectively (Heifetz et al 2009). The pandemic has given us a pause point to reconsider the fundamentals of what universities are really for in whatever lies ahead. So, whilst the pandemic poses huge challenges, it also offers us the opportunity to innovate if we are willing to learn from our experiences. It is essential to learn from this pandemic and not revert to old habits—the rest of the book considers this further.

Chapter 2

Learning and Teaching in Times of Change

Professor Sherif Elsaadany
Professor Judy McKimm

Pandemics have repeatedly contributed to the closure of educational institutions worldwide, with different efficacy levels. For example, many educational institutions in the United States and across the globe have been closed on more than one occasion with both the 1918-19 influenza pandemic and the 2009 H1N1 flu pandemic. Although several countries resort to closing educational institutions to slow the spread of infection, which proves to be a successful policy in general, a study on the closure of educational institutions in Michigan found that *"the interactive closure of educational institutions at the district level was ineffective."* (Frieden 2020; Aiello 2015). This study maintains that closure of educational institutions may succeed in decelerating disease outbreak, providing that the closure decision is made on a timely manner, but if the decision to close is late, efficacy of the closure diminishes if it existed at all. In some cases, higher rates of infection have been reported when schools were reopened after a closure period (Frieden 2020; Aiello 2015).

Originating in the Chinese city of Wuhan, the World Health Organization (WHO) declared the novel coronavirus disease 2019 (COVID-19) a pandemic on 11 March 2020, forcing billions around the world into lockdown. To prevent the outbreak of the disease and to protect staff and students, an increasing number of universities all over the world were required by their governments to cancel or postpone campus-based events. A UNESCO report issued 19 March 2020 claims that this action affected more than half of the total number of enrolled students worldwide. The report further adds that more than 150 countries closed educational institutions completely, something that affected more than 1.19 billion students; meanwhile, other countries have resorted to closing educational institutions only in certain or affected areas. Another UNESCO report released May 25, 2020 maintains that because of the pandemic, 68% of the total number of students worldwide are not enrolled in educational institutions.

The development of a vaccine for COVID-19 is yet come to fruition, therefore the main strategy to date has been to curb the spread of infection and to reduce the pandemic duration and its effects on higher education through social and physical distancing. Many universities have paused formal teaching, which means that there have been no seminars, lectures, or tutorials for some time. As libraries have also been closed, students have been unable to find the required research materials, and therefore examination deadlines have had to be postponed to allow students the time necessary to complete their work. Closure of universities is also a reason that students cannot meet their professors and tutors face-to-face for academic advice or for help with their studies. This poses problems for students who may need supervision for discussing their ideas when writing their Bachelor's or Master's theses and may lead to students being unable to complete their work until they can talk to their advisors (INOMICST Team, 2020).

The UNESCO report in March 2020 maintained that the decision to close educational institutions, be it temporary or not, creates several problems, including the reduction of teaching hours, which affects the academic achievement of students. In addition, there are several difficult-to-measure losses, including financial difficulties incurred by families, as parents are required to balance their work and family obligations. Despite all efforts, this disruption aggravates disparities in the educational system, as richer families are able to afford more resources to maintain a better education, bridge the educational gap, and compensate for their children's inability to go to educational institutions through enrichment activities.

Campus closure and social distancing have been the driving force for universities to adopt more online teaching and assessment approaches. Students undertaking certain topics can have distance study and guidance when campus facilities are not available. Therefore, the main point that needs to be considered is the transition to different learning and assessment methods, and then the impact of this on students, academics and professionals should be assessed. According to Araújo et al. (2020), this raises many unanswered questions, not least what is going to happen to the students whose universities have been affected most severely by the pandemic. In this chapter, we highlight the impacts of COVID-19 on higher education and the need for new management strategies.

The Impact of University Closures

A high social and economic price must be paid for closing educational institutions, even if they are temporary. This includes the potential of amplified pressures on universities that are still open. A 2020 UNESCO report maintains that closure of educational institutions affects all communities, especially disadvantaged groups, from schoolchildren to university students. As they attend centres for human interaction and social activities, university students may not have enough opportunities for development and growth in the face of closure of educational institutions. Not only can they not access their learning, but they may also lose opportunities such as placements and practical training, and they lose social connections that are fundamental to development and wellbeing. Furthermore, the return of students to educational institutions is yet another challenge, particularly if they have been closed for an extended period of time. The following section explains the impact of the closure of educational institutions on students, addressing several key areas.

To guarantee that the education process shall not be interrupted during the temporary closure of educational institutions, UNESCO released a report on 6 March 2020 offering ten recommendations (in bold). These will be explained in the context of learning and teaching in universities.

1. **Examine readiness and choose the most relevant tools.** This recommendation is concerned with making a decision on the use of high-tech and low-tech solutions based on the reliability of local power supplies, internet connectivity, and how advanced are the digital skills of both the teacher and students. The spectrum is wide, ranging from integrated digital learning platforms, through video lessons and MOOCs, to TV and radio broadcasting.

2. **Ensure inclusion of the distance learning programmes.** Measures should be implemented to ensure access to distance learning programmes for all students including those with disabilities or from low-income backgrounds, with possible solutions such as decentralizing tools and devices from computer labs to families on a temporary basis, while supporting the families on the issue of connectivity.

3. **Protect data privacy and data security.** Uploading data or educational resources to web spaces or sharing them with other organizations or individuals, data security should be assessed, while ensuring that students' data privacy shall not be violated by the use of applications and platforms.

4. **Prioritize solutions to address psychosocial challenges before teaching.** All available tools should be mobilized to bring together all stakeholders, such as schools, teachers, parents and students. Virtual communities are vital during isolation periods to ensure interactions, enact measures for social contact, and tackle challenges on the psychosocial level that students may encounter.

5. **Plan the study schedule of the distance learning programmes.** Stakeholders should check possible closure duration of educational institutions and duly examine choices like focusing on teaching new skills and knowledge or augment what the students have already learnt. Several factors should decide the schedule, including the status of the affected areas and the students' level and their needs. Teaching/learning methodologies should be selected according to several factors such as the type of closure and lockdown and the maintenance of a safe physical environment.

6. **Provide support to teachers and parents on the use of digital tools.** Universities need to provide teachers and students with orientation and training sessions when needed. Teachers should be oriented on preparing the basic settings like using internet data in case of live streaming of classes.

7. **Blend appropriate approaches and limit the number of applications and platforms.** For synchronous communication and asynchronous learning, tools or media available for most students should be blended, while avoiding adding more burdens to students by requiring them to download and test several platforms and applications.

8. **Develop distance learning rules and monitor students' learning process.** Rules on distance learning should be decided by involving students. To monitor students' learning process, formative questions, tests, and exercises should be designed, while supporting submission of students' feedback.

9. **Define the duration of distance learning units based on students' self-regulation skills.** Timing should be done according to the level of students' self-regulation and metacognitive abilities, particularly for livestreaming classes. An online class should be carefully structured, and in general, and, in general, should not exceed 20–30 minutes of lecturing time. A longer workshop-type session could be 'chunked' into shorter segments with breaks included to reduce fatigue.

10. **Create communities and enhance connection.** To address the sense of loneliness or helplessness, communities of teachers and school managers should be created to facilitate experience sharing and have discussions on coping strategies when learning difficulties erupt.

The Shift from Face-To-Face to Online Learning

Moving to a completely online delivery of education is a new concept for many teachers and students alike across the globe. However, online learning has existed in universities for a long time, and many faculty members have been trained to use platforms that support online teaching, either as the only delivery mode or within a blended learning approach alongside face-to-face teaching. While Lim (2020) maintains that there is always a possibility that some teachers who are not technology-oriented may not be cope with this mode, some believe otherwise.

Since the start of the pandemic, there has been increased demand for computers and mobile devices at home for those who have to learn or work from home. It can be difficult for faculty to work from home, and this is also coupled with a lack of infrastructure or resources in many universities which do not facilitate an immediate start of online teaching (Dill et al. 2020). Questions raised should be asked about those students who lack access to laptops and internet connectivity at home, the possibility of online teaching of practical courses with, for example, laboratory-based work or music and art, and the status of those students whose classes are impossible to deliver online. Therefore, it is essential that great attention is paid to ensuring the quality of online education.

The most important initial step for all faculty is to understand their institution's content/learning management system (C/LMS) or virtual learning environment (VLE), which provide an online hub for educational resources and communication. Each VLE offers different resources, though most allow for the following functions:

- Content management: A space to store and upload content
- Content planning: A space to map out course structures and timelines
- Progress tracking: A means by which to track student progress
- Communication and collaboration: Environments to share insights, such as emails, notice boards, blogs, wikis, etc.
- Real-time communication: Conferencing via live video or audio
- Assessment: quizzes, submission of assessments, plagiarism software.

When making the shift to an entirely online or a blended learning approach, faculty need to understand not only the simpler functions, such as content management and planning, but also the additional resources that will help to make the online learning experience more dynamic. The potential of online learning is vast as new higher education pathways are introduced and lifelong learning opportunities are extended. Online learning can also help to reduce the costs of education, on individual and institutional levels, by offering low-cost and flexible alternatives. As the pandemic persists, content developers may have a key opportunity to improve quality and boost inclusion in higher education. Digital environments represent a strategic opportunity for different countries to contribute to meeting national learning needs and developing associated potentials. UNESCO has put in place a set of programs to help with distance learning, and some popular VLE digital learning management systems are described in Table 1.

TABLE 2.1 SOME COMMON VIRTUAL LEARNING ENVIRONMENTS (VLES)

PLATFORM	DESCRIPTION
Blackboard	Virtual learning environment and learning management system
Canvas	Learning management platform with integrated products including video, catalogue and portfolio systems
CenturyTech	Personal learning pathways with micro-lessons to address gaps in knowledge, challenge students and promote long-term memory retention
ClassDojo	Connects teachers with students and parents to build classroom communities
Edmodo	Tools and resources to manage classrooms and engage students remotely, offering a variety of languages
Edraak	Arabic language online education with resources for school learners and teachers

EkStep	Open learning platform with a collection of learning resources to support literacy and numeracy
Google Classroom	Helps classes connect remotely, communicate and stay-organized
Moodle	Community-driven and globally-supported open learning platform
Nafham	Arabic language online learning platform hosting educational video lessons that correspond with Egyptian and Syrian curricula
Paper Airplanes	Matches individuals with personal tutors for 12–16-week sessions conducted via video conferencing platforms, available in English and Turkish
Schoology	Tools to support instruction, learning, grading, collaboration and assessment
Seesaw	Enables the creation of collaborative and shareable digital learning portfolios and learning resources
Skooler	Tools to turn Microsoft Office software into an education platform
Zoom	A virtual conference call software that can also be used for teaching

Challenges Facing International Students

Universities worldwide have large numbers of international students, with many partaking in a semester abroad for reasons such as widening their cultural and philological understanding. Some of these students may not be able to travel to their homes during pandemics. A major challenge for administrators is to ensure the delivery of basic services such as accommodation, food and safety to international students.

As universities make the decision to close their campuses and move to online classes, they should consider that those campuses are the home of many international students. Cheng (2020) suggests that even though exceptions are offered for students with additional learning needs, universities often do not pay as much attention to international students, adding that this is problematic, as when they need help, international students can be culturally challenged and sometimes experience racism. As COVID-19 spreads, unconcealed discrimination against international students, especially Asians, have been observed (Ma & Miller, 2020). There is also a lack of institutional efforts in the provision of orientation and educational workshops to deal with such issues.

Bothwell (2020a) lists several problematic issues while the pandemic persists, such as students' need for guidance on how to live in isolation and how to protect themselves from any direct contact. In addition, if examinations are delayed and students have to extend their stay, they may experience financial problems, while those have managed to return to their homes will be concerned about possible interruption of their studies. Another problem is whether students have the right setup at home, including the availability of computers, books, and good internet connectivity. Bothwell suggests that the disruption due to COVID-19 may affect the admissions of international students for the coming academic year (Bothwell, 2020a).

Alston (2020) suggests that the number of international students will decrease as IELTS (International English Language Testing System) and TOEFL (Test of English as a Foreign Language), two of the main providers of English proficiency tests worldwide, have reduced capacity. This will drastically hinder the ability of new students who need to show their proficiency in English to study in that language. Therefore, the number of students whose first language is not English is expected to decrease, because fewer students will be able to provide the certificates they need. In this context, Bothwell (2020a) suggests that lowering English entry requirements should be considered and universities should put in place the means to develop the English language level of the accepted students.

Bothwell stresses that this is not a call for lowering standards, but a call for accepting students who may have failed to gain a certificate in English proficiency and then supporting them in additional ways during the course of their study. Other programmes that rely on global test centres are also affected. For example access to medical programmes often requires applicants to have satisfactorily passed an additional entrance test such as GAMSAT (Graduate Medical Schools Admissions Test) or MCAT (Medical College Admissions Test) and in the US and Canada students at various levels will also have to pass the USMLE (US Medical Licensing Examination) to obtain a postgraduate training post. Admissions and progression may therefore be affected if students cannot take these examinations or they are delayed.

Finally, it is vital that educational institutions maintain communication with students and send them reassuring messages. Universities during the pandemic should offer students flexible solutions, such as offering overseas students who have successfully passed foundation year an option to study remotely for the first year while they are in their countries before returning to the university to continue their studies in subsequent years. Kang et al. (2020) adds that international students live with the fear that their families may be infected with the virus, while they face discrimination and isolation in another country, a situation that may lead to mental health problems, including denial, stress, anxiety, and fear.

Challenges and Strategies for Teachers

In early 2020, as the pandemic surged around the world, many countries went into various forms of lockdown with international students returning to their home countries and home students leaving campus. Prior to this, however universities had already been making plans for campus closure, planning for moving as much teaching and assessment online as possible and facilitating remote working for all faculty, except those who had to be on campus such as security and accommodation staff.

For many programmes, especially those which are more *'knowledge-based'*, the move online was a big burden of work, but possible. However, for programmes with a heavy practical component such as healthcare, biomedical sciences or engineering, it was not possible to provide large parts of some programmes. And in the northern hemisphere, many programmes still had at least three months to run, with assessments due that would contribute towards students' year or final grades.

BOX 2.1   CASE STUDY: A SCIENCE STUDENT'S EXPERIENCE OF COVID-19

As the university closed campus, all classes ended and we were told to study from home. I feel there were a number of things the department and university did well. These included:

- Being very transparent and honest with how the department would go forwards in dealing with the pandemic.
- Providing many updates and notifications mentioning future changes with the course in response to lockdown etc.
- Putting a *"Safety net"* (no detriment policy with regards to grades being affected by COVID-19, i.e. if you did exceptionally poorly due to COVID, your average grades would be taken instead).
- Recording of virtual lectures to allow for more flexibility in student learning.
- Changing examinations to online *"open book"* examinations.

However, some things were not possible or difficult to address:

- Variety in revision materials was lacking due to restricted access to library services.
- Replacements for dissertation projects were lacking. There was no opportunity for students doing completely experimental projects to allow for them to remain within their specialist areas.
- The quality of virtual lectures was poor at first with most lectures having numerous technical issues.
- Support in terms of extensions on projects was variable.
- Many experimental-based modules had to be prematurely rushed/ended, this caused a lot of disruption.

Most of my modules were relatively unaffected by COVID-19, mainly because I mainly chose theoretical modules. However, all of my experimental modules got heavily affected, most got suspended or ended prematurely. A lot of my continuous assessment work was disrupted, and only about 50% of the work I did that should have contributed to my grade actually did. This meant that previously relatively unimportant assessments that I had completed in December suddenly ended up being worth 3 times as much as I had initially anticipated. This heavily skewed some of my modules either positively or negatively and I ended up with grades far less representative of my general skillset.

The impact of the pandemic meant rapid review and reform of policies, processes, regulations and procedures to facilitate a flexible response across the multiple programmes offered by universities: what might work in Chemistry might not work in Art for example. A range of strategies were adopted, depending on the stage of learning/programme, facilities, course content and assessment requirements and learners and teachers' locations. Some practical classes had to be completely cancelled, and as we are thinking about starting a new academic year, plans are now being made around how to catch up missed classes, as well as providing practical teaching in laboratories or on placement when physical distancing measures are in place. This is not without its problems of course; universities will have to be fully prepared for a surge in the virus and potentially more campus closures. What we have learned from this is that flexibility is essential and we cannot simply rely on programme delivery through face to face teaching and large group learning.

So, in planning ahead, we are looking at a much more flexible and blended approach to course delivery, where students can learn online, remotely, then they will probably be safer in the medium term. This might mean that whole programmes are delivered online, and campus attendance will be restricted to those learning activities that require specialised equipment or access to specific facilities. Programmes with a large placement or industry component will need to be adapted, depending on the nature of the learning required. Some courses or modules may not be able to run in the coming academic year, and this may have implications for teacher employment and student enrolment. Some programmes are already being offered at multiple entry points in the year so that universities can attract more students as the course of the pandemic becomes clearer. As educators, we must aim to provide as much certainty as we can for students as to what their course will comprise and how and where they will learn. In high resource settings, we are often fortunate to have robust IT systems, which enables students to have good online access to libraries, learning environments and teachers, this is not the case everywhere and we must not be too ambitious with the tools at our disposal, for example if they require large bandwidth (e.g. streamed videos) then not all students may be able to access these.

The other challenge for teachers is how to balance synchronous (in real time) with asynchronous (learners learn in their own time) learning, especially when learners are in different time zones. Keeping the synchronous learning for discussion, clarification of concepts and small group learning is best, and using a 'flipped classroom' approach where students read and carry out individual activities before meeting synchronously will help keep students motivated and structure their learning. Much planning is needed to provide high quality online learning, but keeping key educational principles in mind will help teachers focus on the needs of the learners more than on the technology available.

BOX 2.2 CASE STUDY: DISTANCE LEARNING AT KING ABDULAZIZ UNIVERSITY

The Coronavirus pandemic was a real test for King Abdulaziz University (KAU), which clearly demonstrated its readiness to deal with exceptional situations that may occur at any moment. The generous and unlimited support of the Saudi government, i.e., the Ministry of Education, has all the credit in developing an advanced infrastructure and high-efficiency training for its cadres. This has enabled the University to make a complete and smooth transformation from face-to-face education to distance education just one day after the issuance of the transformation directives by His Excellency the Minister of Education. During the pandemic, the University was able to implement proactive emergency plans, which have been built on monitoring data, needs and expectations. This enabled the University to continue the educational process in a safe environment, while maintaining efficiency and quality, to guarantee educational achievement for all students.

The optimal use of the virtual classroom platform (BlackBoard) during the Coronavirus pandemic is one of the success stories of KAU. BlackBoard statistics show that it was used over 1.700.000 times, with over 82 000 shared files, over 141.000 sessions and over 484 000 electronic assessments over all programs. Also, over 140 seminars were held, at least 270 scientific theses were defended, more than 85 training courses were provided to faculty and students, and the technical support team tackled over 52.000 requests. In addition, a huge academic archive of virtual lectures was recorded during the pandemic period. The upsurge in the number of evaluations that aim to measure the achievement of the learning outcomes indicates an increase in the technical and academic readiness of faculty and students in distance learning training programs to use distance learning applications and practices. This has improved the skills of both students and staff to better use e-learning methods to cope with the latest updates in the field.

The University faced some serious challenges, and perhaps it is worthy to mention two of them. The first was the sudden increase of the technical support requests, but the problem was solved by increasing the number of technical support staff while distributing them at shifts covering all times of morning and evening virtual classes. The second challenge was the immediate need to train fresh students, students with special needs, and newly appointed faculty members to use the virtual classroom platform. The university increased the numbers and types of courses on special topics to train about 16 000 beneficiaries. Special virtual courses and classes were devoted to the people with additional learning needs.

We foresee that in the future, distance education shall be connected to higher education worldwide, as there will be great interest to achieve the following:

- An approach to provide university educational programs as distance education, in either full or part, to achieve the optimal investment of educational resources.
- Developing educational programs that focus on labour market needs and use distance education technologies and practices to reach the largest possible segment of beneficiaries and therefore boost equal opportunities in education. education, along with its practices and applications, shall be one of the most important higher education strategies in Saudi universities that aim to provide high quality education and increase the financial feasibility of resources.

Faculty development was provided at rapid pace to help teachers adapt their teaching and learning to online formats. Many teachers had previously only used their university's VLE (Blackboard™, Moodle™, Canvas™ etc.) as a content repository for lectures or other resources, or for students to submit assignments. Suddenly, whilst working from their living rooms or home offices (if they were lucky) they were expected to provide teaching and other activities for their students using software and apps they had never used before, such as Zoom™.

What is really heartening however, is that because everyone is in a similar position, educators around the world were very willing to share their challenges, ideas and tips. For a description on how an international group of health professions' educators recognised the need for mutual support and came together to mentor one another and share practice and ideas through virtual webinars and workshops, search for the ***Mentors without borders*** blogpost online.

Summary

An unprecedented and global situation such as the coronavirus naturally brings forward a myriad of worries and impacts. This chapter has summarised the impact of university closures on both faculty and students. To mitigate the impacts of university closures, Reimers and Schleicher (2020, pp.5–6) have proposed a 25-point checklist for an educational response to the pandemic (see Annex 1). These points can be a tool for university leaders and serve as managing strategies that broadly align with the UNESCO goals outlined above. They emphasise the need to prioritise the health and safety of students and faculty while ensuring delivery of educational content. Furthermore, they suggest reprioritising curriculum goals, identifying the means of education delivery and ensuring adequate support for teachers and students. Finally, they stress the need for communication, collaboration, and mutual support between faculty, students, and stakeholders.

Chapter 3

Assessment during COVID-19

Professor Sherif Elsaadany
Professor Abdulmonem Al-Hayani

It is clear that the current coronavirus outbreak has significantly disrupted the higher education sector. Travel bans and campus closures have forced many students and teaching staff across the world into varying degrees of isolation, presenting serious barriers to the teaching and learning process. As a result, universities across the world have been making their own decisions regarding examinations. Some have resorted to online examinations, while others have postponed or cancelled them altogether. According to Timmis et al. (2016), as some universities suspend their final examinations, continuous assessment processes continue with online classes.

It must be noted that although assessments and evaluation are seriously affected by the transition to online teaching, assessment and evaluation are usually underdeveloped compared to teaching and learning processes, which have a better technological support. The development of online assessments for courses designed for face-to-face learning is a challenge, as procedures to administer projects and assessments in general are not clear for both students and faculty (Raaheim et al., 2019).

Furthermore, moving to an online mode requires changing assessment types, as online invigilation is difficult, and this raises the issue of ensuring that students do not cheat during online assessments (Alruwais et al., 2018). It is also stated that it is impossible to conduct certain classes online, such as practical sessions, laboratory tests, performance tests, and others. Finally, there are disadvantages for students who lack internet connectivity and they may suffer from online assessments, which may affect their marks. This chapter discusses these issues in detail.

Electronic assessment (e-Assessment)

The learning process has been well developed following the introduction of electronic learning and assessment. According to Gilbert et al. (2011), e-assessment enhances the process of measuring learning outcomes (LOs) in addition to allowing students to receive direct and immediate feedback for their performance. It is essential to create an assessment system while keeping in mind educational goals and enhancing the skills of students. Ridgway (2004) claims that e-assessment may come in several types: automatic administrative procedures, digitizing paper-based systems and online testing including multiple-choice tests and assessment of problem-solving skills. E-assessment is therefore a process in which all assessments are electronic and dependent on the latest technology. This includes every step of the assessment process, such test design, application, test-taking, and feedback. A framework designed by Whitelock (2006) allows faculty members to address the barriers and the cultural debate surrounding e-assessment strategies. Whitelock stresses the significance of motivation as the cycle's first step, as motivation to undertake this drives the whole process. The next steps include assessment design, creation, testing students, delivery of outcomes, data retrieval and processing so that feedback is gained, evaluation of outcomes, and finally review of the feedback. Based on the data received from the evaluation of outcomes and feedback, the cycle returns to the design and creation steps and starts over again to improve the assessment and feedback processes and to ensure that course objectives are met and desired outcomes are reached.

Methods of Assessment in Online Learning

The literature on methods, types and distribution of assessment in online learning less well-developed than that relating to face-to-face assessment. One early attempt, conducted by Swan (2001), examined 73 online courses and identifies several assessment methods included discussions, written assignments, projects, quizzes, tests and group work. The study found that around 75% of the courses consider online discussion a graded activity, while around 50% of the courses adopt written assignments and tests as a method of assessment. Similar findings were reported in a subsequent study conducted by Arend (2007), where 60 online courses were examined, and the most common assessment methods identified were online discussions, examinations, written assignments, experimental assignments, problem assignments, quizzes, journals, projects, and presentations. This study also found that the majority of the courses also consider online discussion a graded activity. The study further reported out that 83% of the courses depend on quizzes and tests and 63% of the courses use written assignments.

Gaytan and McEwen (2007), in their work on identifying effective methods of assessment for online courses, found that they include projects, portfolios, self-assessments, tests and quizzes, asynchronous discussion, and peer evaluations, sometimes with feedback. While the researchers recommend utilising several assignments, they stress the significance of a timely feedback and examining the written record of students, such as discussions and e-mails, to keep well-informed on their needs and concerns. This research shows the range of types of assessments that can be used in e-learning, which may be overwhelming to both faculty and students. The questions are: what are the advantages of e-assessment, and how do we choose the right type?

Advantages of e-assessment

E-assessment provides several advantages for educators and students, supported by a range of studies:

- E-assessment is a flexible tool that students in remote areas can use and have assessments any time in their own environment (Williams, 2009)
- Instant feedback helps improve the learning process
- Students see e-assessment as fast and friendly, with the process resembling gaming and recreational activities (Eljinini, 2012)
- A study conducted with Glamorgan University and Leeds Metropolitan University suggested that e-assessment improves student performance (Gilbert, 2011)
- This supports the findings of Marriott (2009) in a study conducted in University of Winchester that found that e-assessment increases motivation, and in turn enhances performance
- A survey-based study found that e-assessment is preferred by 88.4% of students compared to traditional testing (Donovan, 2007)
- This was further supported by a study by Llamas-Nistal et al. (2013) who found that 43 out of 52 students preferred e-assessment to traditional examinations.
- In a survey study on Jordan University and Zayed University, Tubaishat (2006) found that 59% and 50% of students, respectively, prefer e-assessment.
- According to Sorensen (2013), students value the role of e-assessment in their learning process, which is further supported by Gilbert (2011) who found that 92% of the students agree that e-assessment boosts their learning.

A study conducted in Leeds Metropolitan University found that educators feel that e-assessment helps save time, effort and money (Sorensen, 2013). E-assessment may help improve the quality of feedback (Ridgway, 2004) and due to the direct feedback from the multiple e-assessments during the course, teachers can track and analyse the performance of students to tackle problems before final examinations (Ellaway, 2008). Finally, e-assessment also helps in assessing courses with large numbers of students.

Instead of traditional paper examinations, universities adopt e-assessment for faster and more accurate assessment methods. In fact, the efficacy of e-assessment can even help universities assess new applicants in a cost-effective and timesaving way (Ridgway, 2004). With regards to testing, e-assessment is more accurate than paper tests in determining the level of students, as it can change the difficulty level of questions in an assessment according to the response of students—known as adaptive testing. Furthermore, Eljinini (2012) mentions that security measures in e-assessment limit a student's ability to cheat, for example by changing the order of questions and preventing copying questions. Security measures also include checking identity and password verification.

Thus, e-assessment can be a tool used by universities and provides several advantages and is looked upon favourably by both teachers and students. It can help in achieving education goals as it supports high skills of thinking, i.e., critique thinking, and this reflects on cognitive processes of learning and helps accelerate collective projects. E-assessment also helps to focus on problem-solving solutions with the help of computers, especially in science and mathematics.

Assessment Challenges in Online Learning

The move to e-assessment in university examinations is not an easy task. This could help to explain why several universities appear to be holding off cancelling examinations in the hope that by the time of final examinations, COVID-19 restrictions will be lifted. One of the challenges online instructors need to address is how to convey their messages to students accurately without face-to-face contact, and subsequently provide students with the appropriate feedback so that students may be able to achieve the targeted LOs. According to Way (2012), the nature of online learning adds difficulty to assessments, especially for those who lack computer devices or good internet connections. The lack of direct contact and unfamiliarity with e-assessment technology poses extra burdens on online instructors (Oncu & Cakir, 2011). Beebe et al. (2012) studied the e-assessment concerns of a group of instructors who moved their traditional classes to online classes, and found that instructors have five areas of concern: time management, student responsibility and initiative, structure of online medium, complexity of content, and informal assessment.

E-assessment is more effective in the types of questions with well-defined answers, and for examinations requiring complex or subjective answers, immediate computerised scoring may not be possible. A solution for the problem of scoring and correcting questions in an online environment is to correlate the scores of computer and human judges, and then the scores of two human judges (Ridgway, 2004). Using this method, in a study in Dundee Medical School, Mitchell et al. (2003) found that human scoring time was greatly reduced, while the quality of the questions was improved. However, this approach can be time-consuming, especially at first. When tackling the issue of assessment of group work and projects, the tasks need several factors such as evaluating interpersonal and communication skills, group activity, and feedback, among others (Ridgway, 2004). Although e-assessment is hard to use in these tasks, an academic open-source template, known as SPARK (Self Peer Assessment Resource Kit) has been introduced and has proved successful in different university contexts.

For further reading on other issues covered in the review of literature on e-assessment, such as the significance of authentic assessment, use of assessments to stimulate academic self-regulation, concerns over academic integrity, assessing online collaboration and discussions, see Kim et al., (2008), Simonson et al. (2006), and Naismith et al., 2011.

Maintaining Academic Integrity in a Digital Context

Assessment can be compromised, unfortunately, by cheating and plagiarism. Ensuring that grades awarded in 2020 carry the same value as previous years is a key objective in the COVID-19 crisis. This leads us to discuss academic integrity, which is often meant to support students and preclude academic misconduct. It has several elements such as principles, values, conduct, measures and systems relevant to fairness and honesty in all aspects of the academic process, such as teaching, learning and assessment. Mostrous and Kenber (2016) state that however the assessments are carried out, academic institutions must maintain academic integrity in their approaches to quality and standards.

Studies suggest that students cheat for several reasons, such as lacking support, lack of adequate research skills, confidence, interest, engagement with studies, and time management skills, among others. In a crisis such as COVID-19, more students may cheat or draw on services such as essay mills. Recently, essay mills have increased in popularity, and have propagated widely, where individuals or organizations contract students to do their projects or assignments for a fee.

They also offer other services, such as assigning someone to complete online examinations and project reports. These are obviously controversial, with some institutions considering them forms of cheating and/or plagiarism; however, some argue that there is no legislation prohibiting the use of contract cheating services (Glendinning, 2017). Newton (2015) claims that cheating, as a behaviour, may be an acquired habit and students may not understand the inappropriateness and consequences of such a behaviour. Lancaster and Draper (2020) note that students who learn at a distance may feel less supported compared to regular times, and duly they may have additional motivations to cheat. Furthermore, more attention should be paid to international students who may face language problems and lack understanding of assignment requirements.

Technological tools can help detecting plagiarism and academic misconduct but they should not be regarded as solutions, rather as a support tool for detection and prevention. Although such technological tools include text matching software that can discover copied texts, they are of little help to detect essays written by essay mills, which sometimes offer plagiarism-free work. Also available are analytics software that detect writing style variations and suggests whether the work submitted is written by a single author. Other software includes stylometrics tools, which can track writing and linguistic styles. In an attempt to tackle the problem of remote invigilation for online examinations, some universities install webcams and facial recognition software to student computers, but this step should be taken with the approval of students as it can lead to privacy concerns and legal problems. This stresses the importance of keeping everyone in the academic community aware of the latest academic regulations applicable to assessments and maintaining the required standards of academic integrity.

Draper et al. (2017) state that some instructors shorten the allowed time to complete and submit assignments to minimize cheating, yet this view becomes less prevalent as essay mills are always ready to offer their paid services in high quality and short notice. One solution for this issue is to set checkpoints for an assignment, such as discussing the first draft and debating the findings in order to detect and reduce possibilities of cheating. In this context, Beckman and Lam (2016) suggest that educational institutions may block internet access to essay mills from campus facilities, while sending a warning message to any user who may attempt to access them, with a reminder that this is against academic integrity guidelines. Dawson (2017) suggests interviewing the student after assessing an assignment to detect if a third party is involved in answering the assignment. Although this viva assessment technique is common in higher education, it is impractical to adopt for every student and every assignment, and therefore random sampling is suggested as a deterrent. While interviewing students to defend their opinions can be useful, another indicator of cheating is observing a sharp discrepancy between a student's grades in different assessments.

Overall, maintaining academic integrity is at the heart of all educational systems, and must not be forgotten in the midst of crises such as this pandemic. When thinking of solutions to minimize cheating, course developers should be cautious in their e-assessment design. Newton (2015) suggests that one solution could be changing assessment questions from objective measures (MCQs and true-false questions) to subjective (essay questions and research). Open source or open book examinations also can be helpful in their requirement for students to demonstrate 'application' of knowledge to a question or topic rather than simple recall which can tempt students to cheat without invigilation. Devising questions that require a thorough perception of the topic and individual development of arguments is more clearly linked to real life and requires more advanced learning skills from students.

Faculty may then use plagiarism detection software tools when they review research papers and essay questions. However, they must bear in mind that these tools are not perfect. Mission statements and values of educational institutions should signal association with academic integrity, which must be clearly reflected in regulations in different languages and forms. Universities must also put into place mechanisms to report a suspicion of academic misconduct. Designated academic conduct officials could deal with routine issues of academic integrity, while complex issues of academic misconduct and appeals should be referred to a panel consisting of well-trained and supported officials. Records of cheating incidents and academic misconduct should be maintained for analysis to find appropriate solutions. Overall, maintaining academic integrity requires a systematic approach.

Recommendations

The following recommendations could help mitigate assessment issues during the global pandemic:

- Written assignments with complex nature that require synthesizing materials from the entire semester could be divided into phases and students may submit interim deliverables to receive feedback. For example, a paper could be submitted in three phases: (a) context description; (b) problem analysis; and (c) recommendations. However, feedback is significant, though labour-intensive. One suggestion is to put in place rubrics to be used by students as guidelines, and this may be supplemented with examples of previous student work. Students may also have the opportunity to comment on one another's work.

- Rubrics can be used as guides for student activities, either on discussion boards or in written assignments. A rubric may come in different forms and the simplest is to be a checklist specifying criteria of target performance. Developing the rubric ahead of time may help stipulating the objectives of the assignment. When students use the rubric while working on the assignment, they can understand what they are expected to do and adjust their performance. Once the rubric is developed, the grading system for each step could be put in place. Rubrics for online discussions may include points like the frequency of a student's posts, replies, relevance to course content, among others.

- Self-check quizzes are an effective tool in dense and technical courses as they force students to complete the required readings and assess how far they understand the material. Most platforms of content management systems have a mechanism for deploying such quizzes, and faculty may check available features in the platform on hand. Many platforms offer automated feedback, whether immediate or at set time/date.

- Synchronous technologies are useful when used appropriately, as many of the challenges online instructors face are the result of the distant, asynchronous nature of most online learning. To help close this gap, online and phone conferencing can be used. However, conferencing has its problems too, including ability of all students to attend at the same time and the possibility that international students are in multiple time zones. Therefore, sessions should be recorded, and session schedules could be changed every week. Student presentations could be done using web conferencing at the end of the semester, and scheduling several sessions, each at a different time, could be a solution.

- Peer-assessment strategies can be used to promote community development and allow students to learn through analysing and critiquing the work of their peers, but it is worth mentioning that rubrics are a must for such activities. Rubrics help students specify the target performance criteria and they deconstruct a task into smaller subtasks, making it easier to assess and criticize their peers' works. Peer assessment is suitable for written assignments that have interim deliverables. Finally, students may be interested in viewing their peers' work, and it may encourage deeper thinking, sharing of ideas, and collaboration.

- To reduce the time spent repeating the same feedback for each student, appropriate opportunities should be seized to address the entire class. In a big assignment, faculty members may post a summary of the trends and common mistakes in the submissions and make recommendations for what is expected in the next step.

Every educational institution should be encouraged to adopt a strategy that integrates a culture of academic integrity and discouraging academic misconduct in all its forms. This strategy should be clearly set in strong, consistent, and transparent policies that stipulate punitive actions for any violation. It is of a paramount significance that student have written and oral information on the importance of academic integrity and the educational institution's stance. Students need to know that the educational institution use text-matching software, which may discourage students to cut and paste, or to contract essay mills as they may be caught. Some universities ask students to sign declarations that their submitted work is authentic and plagiarism-free, but this may not prevent cheating and dishonesty; however, it may prompt the message of the importance of honesty and highlight consequences of cheating. Students need also to receive support to gain necessary study skills such as academic writing, using academic sources, referencing, paraphrasing, and research. These skills are crucial for the students to succeed without cheating. Therefore, mechanisms for maintaining and enhancing academic integrity should be seen as an integral part of the quality assurance process of the educational institution so that it can be scrutinized, monitored and reviewed regularly.

Chapter 4

Nurturing and Sustaining Learner and Faculty Wellbeing

Professor Judy McKimm

The COVID-19 pandemic has been a major disruption for all those who work in and study at universities around the world. This disruption has led to great change and uncertainty for many, including moving into various levels and stages of lockdown and social distancing, rapid adaptations being made to educational provision, and major psychological and physical adaptations occurring in people's lives. In this chapter we consider what the concept of 'wellbeing' means in practice to universities, why it is important, and the issues the pandemic has thrown up in terms of supporting wellbeing. We then consider some of the challenges and strategies involved in supporting faculty and students returning to campus and some of the lessons learned that we might take forward to future practice.

Wellbeing is not easy to define (Dodge et al 2012), but it is essentially:

> *an internal feeling relating to the experience of health, happiness, and prosperity. It includes having good mental health, high life satisfaction, a sense of meaning or purpose, and ability to manage stress. More generally, wellbeing is just feeling well.*

Five main types of wellbeing have been identified:

1. Emotional Wellbeing: the ability to practice stress-management techniques, be resilient, and generate the emotions that lead to good feelings
2. Physical Wellbeing: The ability to improve the functioning of your body through healthy eating and good exercise habits
3. Social Wellbeing: The ability to communicate, develop meaningful relationships with others, and maintain a support network that helps you overcome loneliness
4. Workplace Wellbeing: The ability to pursue your interests, values, and purpose in order to gain meaning, happiness, and enrichment professionally
5. Societal Wellbeing: The ability to actively participate in a thriving community, culture, and environment.

(Rath et al 2010)

The Importance of Wellbeing in the University Setting

Universities have a responsibility for the physical and psychological safety of their learners and faculty. This means that universities need to provide services which help nurture and sustain the wellbeing of those who study and work there (Vogan et al 2014). Such services typically include:

- Health and safety – this includes services for everyone, such as workstation needs, laboratory, buildings and fire safety, and for some may include occupational health support, for example if they have been ill and are returning to work or study, or work on computers a lot and need an eye test.
- Disability or additional learning needs – these services are for learners (and faculty) who have a registered or confirmed physical or behavioural disability (such as dyslexia, dyspraxia, wheelchair user, impaired hearing or sight) so that they can receive the support they need to study or work effectively.

- Wellbeing – in many universities, there will be somewhere students and staff can go for confidential help and guidance around managing stress, mental health and wellbeing. This might include help for students on managing their studies or revising for examinations, counselling services or mindfulness training.

- Sport and recreation – maintaining physical health is very important and universities usually encourage and facilitate students and faculty to participate in activities, providing sports facilities (gyms, swimming pools, sports pitches) and cycle to work schemes or fitness sessions.

- Accommodation, finance, registry and administration– these general support services provide students with access to general enquiries about their programmes, as well as a wider range of services, such as helping them find accommodation or guiding students to bursaries or scholarships. Programme-specific administrative and academic services are also in place to support students.

- Pastoral or personal tutors and workplace mentors – most universities have a system of providing more tailored support for students through personal tutors who have an allocated group of students from their programme who they support and advise. For staff, mentoring schemes, particularly for new or junior staff, can help them make adjustments and transitions.

All these services are designed to ensure that everyone in universities can feel safe and thrive. They are supported by systems, policies and processes which operate to maintain stability and certainty, even during times of emergency, such as a fire or an individual accident or illness. However, the pandemic has led to a potential crisis that requires deft action by universities, set within a context of great uncertainty, fear and anxiety.

Issues and Challenges Raised by the Pandemic

The main challenges around wellbeing include assuring the physical and psychological safety of faculty and learners as many people began to work remotely or experience online learning and communicating, see Box 4.1.

BOX 4.1   CASE STUDY: KING ABDULAZIZ UNIVERSITY'S (KAU) EXPERIENCE OF MAINTAINING STUDENTS' WELLBEING DURING THE COVID-19 PANDEMIC

During the pandemic, students everywhere were exposed to severe psychological traumas and disturbances in their daily life. In addition, their mode of study was suddenly completely shifted from face-to-face to online education. This disturbed their academic and social lives and extracurricular activities, as lockdown was enforced for 15 hours a day in most areas of Saudi Arabia and around the clock in some cities and neighbourhoods.

Once the crisis began to unfold, KAU gathered pace to develop a comprehensive plan to address possible problems and to maintain staff and students' wellbeing at different levels: academic, psychological, social, technical, and even financial. The plan depended mainly on collaborative work between different deanships in the University, namely, the dean of e-learning and distant education, the dean of student affairs and the dean of admission and registration. The dean of e-learning and distant education provided many supportive measures for students to facilitate their online study, with a special focus on how to deal with the new methods of online assessment using the BlackBoard platform. The dean also developed and disseminated many student guidelines and brochures on how to use different tools on BlackBoard and virtual classrooms. In addition, several orientation videos were developed and technical support services were available around the clock.

The dean of student affairs offered students immense psychological support through online lectures, webinars, videos, flyers, and a 24-hour hotline to deal with students' psychological problems and anxiety due to the pandemic. The mode was changed from face-to-face to online in almost every aspect of student life: from online classes through to online academic counselling and online office hours. International students and students who live in university accommodation were given special care, especially in the Moslem fasting month Pof Ramadan. This included providing breakfast meals, health care services, and some social activities while maintaining all necessary protective measures. The dean of student affairs also offered financial support to the more vulnerable students who needed laptops, especially students living far from home and in university accommodation.

The dean of admission and registration played a vital role to counter the negative effects of the pandemic on students and staff. Moving from face-to-face to online education, the deanship made swift changes in students' schedules and assessment methods on very short notice. One of the challenges was dealing with courses with large numbers of students, as university servers may not provide the service as required under such immense pressure, and therefore students were divided into smaller groups. This smooth transition from direct to online education was also accompanied by reviewing and rescheduling assessments, thanks to the close collaboration between the dean of admissions and registration, the dean of e-learning and distant education, and the dean of information technology.

We feel that KAU succeeded during the pandemic to maintain students' wellbeing. One of the most important keys of success was the harmony between all university sectors, deanships and colleges, supported and orchestrated by the higher university administration. Overall, the university's president, vice-presidents and deans were role models as both leaders and managers in the stressful period of the pandemic.

The 'COINNS' framework (McKimm 2008) can be used to pose questions about the main challenges universities are experiencing at any moment, whether this is in 'crisis' mode or for the longer term, and help guide what is needed to ensure continuity of university life, of programmes, learning and teaching and processes for leaders, administrators, faculty, the university and students. Some questions around maintaining physical and psychological safety include consideration of the needs of various groups and services:

- How do we help: people staying on campus; faculty starting remote working; students starting to learn remotely and/or move home, maybe overseas; students staying on campus or who might be isolated?
- How will we know if someone is struggling?
- How can we continue to provide central and support services?

- What is essential, what can we stop, what consequences might there be if we stop or reduce services?
- How will we ameliorate or deal with a crisis?

COINNS also asks us to consider ideas. Universities will not have all the answers themselves and in times of crisis it is essential to move quickly. So they need to reach out and discuss with others around the world what strategies are working and share practices and ideas. It is important to learn from others as the pandemic moves through its various stages in different countries. As McKimm et al (2020) suggest, some of the learning lessons that were quickly learned by educators in relation to coping during the pandemic were that safety is paramount, communication and transparency is key and to acknowledge the need for psychological adaptation to change and crisis. We will discuss these aspects in relation to wellbeing next.

Safety Is Paramount, Communication and Transparency Is Key

At the crisis stage of the pandemic, universities had to pay close attention to ensuring staff and students' physical safety, as this was paramount. Strategies for ensuring physical safety involve practical steps such as deciding how physical distance and flow around and within buildings should occur, how wellbeing, occupational health, disability and other support services will work, and whether, when and how staff and students will return to campus. Closing campuses and cancelling classes were the main ways that this was achieved in the early stages. However, in relation to wellbeing this may have caused more problems than solutions.

If we consider the list of services above, it is clear that some services may stop completely such as sports facilities without too much detriment. Other services, such as building safety, may be primarily addressed by closing buildings related to teaching, learning and research, although some (such as laboratories carrying out vital research) may stay open but with restrictions. As universities start to reopen their campuses, even meeting people's basic physical safety needs will become challenging. Universities have taken different approaches to this. Many have decided to keep learning and teaching online until the situation becomes clearer and hope that students will still decide to attend university.

Others have taken a more blended approach, for example:

- Maintaining physical distance in lecture theatres, laboratories and other spaces between individuals
- Providing hand sanitisers, and other disinfectants
- 'Zoning' various groups of staff and students into different physical spaces ('bubbles') so they cannot intermingle
- Bringing various groups of students onto campus at different stages
- Allowing staff to work remotely for some or all of the time.

Of course, some faculty and students may also contract the coronavirus and these issues will have to be addressed on a case-by-case basis, but there must be a mechanism by which cases can be reported and recorded, especially when everyone returns to campus.

Maintaining effective and timely communication when faculty are working remotely and students have returned home is a major challenge, particularly in terms of the wider organisation and its leadership and management. Managing uncertainty in a daily-changing external environment requires developing effective and frequent communication routes among teachers and learners.

Robust digital services are vital when face-to-face communication cannot happen but we have to be realistic about their benefits and limitations. As well as shifting to learning online, students will also be worried about accommodation, their finances, progression or graduation, visas and cannot access the host of advice provided by departments and individuals that is normally easily accessible to them on campus. Making sure students have clarity about how and who to access is therefore important.

Virtual technologies are not so helpful in terms of maintaining wellbeing as they are for other forms of communication, particularly in relation to struggles with mental health or motivation. It can be hard to fully engage people and it is much easier for individuals to 'hide', or fail to respond, when they are not meeting face-to-face. Setting up regular communications (email, phone, video-meeting) with those for whom you are responsible plus identifying and setting up virtual 'drop in' sessions can help people to continue to engage.

Acknowledge the Need for Psychological Adaptation to Change and Crisis

We also need to think about an individual's psychological needs, particularly when they perceive something as a crisis (Kim and Cameron 2011). For example, Abraham Maslow identified that humans have a range of needs, and if these are not met then they cannot fully function and become what is called *'self-actualised'* (Maslow 1981). Another way of thinking about human needs which is more focused on psychological and self-fulfilment aspects has been described by Tony Robbins who suggests that humans have six main needs. The four needs of the personality:

1. *Certainty*
2. *Variety*
3. *Significance*
4. *Connection/love*

And the two needs of the spirit:

1. *Growth*
2. *Contribution*

(Robbins, 2014)

This helpful framework reminds us that every individual (whether staff or student) needs to have some certainty about their particular situation, so regular, clear communications are vital. However, when people are working or studying remotely, they also need some variety in their activities and to feel that they 'belong' and are connected to others (Thompson 2020). In both Robbins' and Maslow's frameworks, both during and after the initial crisis stage, universities need to pay attention to supporting people's psychological wellbeing. People need to feel as if they are making a significant contribution, that they belong to a cohort, team or group, that they are accomplishing things and receiving feedback (to help boost their self-esteem), and that they are being stretched to reach their potential. So, what does this mean in practice? For learners (and teachers), it is not enough for everything to simply be posted online or for them to participate in passive Zoom™ webinar after Zoom webinar for hours, or they risk becoming bored and disengaged. And as students and staff return to campus, care will need to be taken to balance these needs with maintaining physical safety.

During the pandemic, this may involve helping and supporting people to cope with change and uncertainty, such as allaying student and faculty fears, supporting them to change behaviours to work effectively from home, or looking after and supporting students who are isolated away from home, or who have returned home and are now at a distance (Magallanes 2020). No one can study, work or function well if they are anxious, stressed or coping with great uncertainty. In what humans perceive to be a crisis or emergency, the brain functions less from the cognitive processing areas in the cerebral cortex, but instead the more *'primitive'* part of the brain (the amygdala) kicks in and responses can be more emotional and reactive than intellectual. This is why regular communications are essential, as leaders must make time to listen and not dismiss people's concerns or what might seem to be overly emotive responses. Everyone is different and wellbeing rests on healthy cognitive functions.

Another way we can look at how people respond to change draws from the way people process grief and loss. Any change involves both losses and gains. Even a positive change (such as having a new baby or moving house) involves some loss of what was in the past. As humans process the impact of change on themselves and those around them they require time to move through various stages (Kubler-Ross and Kessler, 2009). This processing generates both emotional and rational responses, and the work of leaders, managers and teachers is to help people work through those stages until they see the change as more positive than negative and they are accepted as the 'new normal'. We talk more about this in Chapter 6.

In relation to COVID-19, we saw how shocked or disbelieving people were at the beginning of the pandemic until they saw the impact on their lives. Then responses became more emotional (anger, blame, bargaining) as campuses emptied and many people moved or began to work from home, asking questions such as *'what will happen to my course?'*, *'will I be able to graduate/progress?'*, *how will I work while I am looking after children at home?*.

For countries where lockdown or strict curfews lasted for weeks, apathy set in: *'will it always be like this?'* Teachers and managers need to look out for people and check in regularly to make sure that people are not shifting from 'normal' anxiety or low mood to clinical depression (Moir et al 2018). The mental health and wellbeing services that support students and staff need to work in a very different way to enable rapid response, virtual consultations and online resources. And face-to-face consultations need to be available for those in severe distress. Teachers or line managers need to be aware of referral processes as they may change during the pandemic.

Gradually, people start to see potential gains, such as having more flexibility when working from home, losing a long commute, or not having to sit in crowded lecture theatres. They might explore options, start to be more creative and then they move towards accepting the 'new reality' for what it is, looking to the future rather than dwelling on the past, and eventually performing optimally.

Learning and Working Remotely

As many countries are shifting to remote digital management systems, home working and online learning, a robust technological infrastructure is essential. However, these can lead to issues for students and staff around wellbeing. People may not have good access to the technology they need or connections may be poor.
Working remotely and in isolation, perhaps with family present or no space to work and study, can be very stressful and therefore individuals need support to maintain motivation and engagement. We cannot assume everyone has the ability or motivation to work or learn in this way and attending (and concentrating on) one after another Zoom meeting or teaching session definitely takes its toll on physical as well as mental health.

Managing workload is also difficult as home/work boundaries slip into one another (particularly if people have other duties such as clinical work or family responsibilities) and not everyone is suited to working like this (Inceoglu and Warr 2011; Lent and Schwartz 2012). Some personality types (such as the *sociable introvert*) are much more suited than others to working in isolation. Many faculty lack confidence and competence in providing online learning, both technically and pedagogically, and even those experienced with online education can feel they are adapting learning and teaching activities 'on the fly', with insufficient time to prepare and develop high quality learning activities. But full engagement with online technologies is more complicated than one single factor. Maican et al's (2019) study found that:

'the use of online communication and collaboration applications is not a single factor predicting success in academic life, but the use of technology combined with high levels of work engagement, consciousness, emotional stability, openness, extraversion and confidence in one's ability to cope with new technologies could increase the chances of success'.

Students who are struggling academically or who cannot continue their studies or research may be very stressed and anxious and, if they were relying on boosting their grades in a final year or module examination, or their viva was delayed, they may feel disappointed, even angry. If assessments are essential and they have to be run online, then this raises issues in terms of practicalities of running the assessments, ensuring access to the assessment is fair and equitable (with regard to time zones, devices, a quiet space, web access and bandwidth) as well as ensuring that students are behaving with integrity and not cheating.

These assessment changes can be very stressful for students and teachers will need to be as flexible and supportive as possible, within the regulations. As a specific example, the UK Government has put this general advice for students on its website: 'many students will be feeling uncertain and anxious and it is vital that they can still access the mental health support they need.

The Government has told Vice-Chancellors to prioritise this and many universities are bolstering their existing mental health services and adapting them in the absence of face-to-face support. Students who are struggling with their mental health at this time can also access online resources from Public Health England, along with online support from the NHS and mental health charity *Mind*.

Conclusions

Decisions will need to be made, and kept under continual review, around maintaining essential services related to wellbeing, in the context of government and local guidance. The pandemic will occur in waves and so, when re-occupation of buildings and campuses is being considered, physical safety is paramount and maintaining social distancing for staff and students, as well as being vigilant for outbreaks of the virus (and other diseases), is vital. Being able to provide access to cafes and other food outlets will also need to be managed. It may be that re-opening sports and exercise facilities are later priorities. For individuals with disabilities, additional considerations may need to be considered.

Alongside physical safety, maintaining the other aspects of wellbeing need to be embedded into the fabric of university life. Many of the typical university structures and societies which enable social, societal and workplace wellbeing may not be able to function as before. For students who had to leave without graduating or saying goodbye to friends and teachers or for new students planning to start a course, their experiences are not what they might have expected.

Whilst activities such as virtual graduations or other ceremonies cannot replace the real thing, they can help compensate for students and teachers' losses by recognising achievements, fostering belonging and a sense of community and enriching lives. Similarly, thinking about how new and returning students can be welcomed into the university as a community whilst maintaining safety is very important. Universities therefore need to be as clear as they can, provide timely and regular communications, and keep a focus on all aspects of wellbeing, as without this, no one can learn, work or thrive.

Chapter 5

Supporting Research Activities during the Pandemic

Professor Ayman Elsamanoudy
Dr Mohammed Hassanien
Dr Sameh Salah Youssef

With the emerging coronavirus (COVID-19) pandemic in 2020, nearly all countries across the world have experienced some form of forced lockdown of all except essential services, such as food supply shops and health and social care services. Although in some cases the ability to collect data is still available, many scientists have not been able to access their equipment or workspaces, resulting in the interruption of many research projects (Saraswat 2020).

Research Topics During the COVID-19 Pandemic

The impact of the COVID-19 lockdown on research has been immense and has led to many challenges. Many adverse outcomes of the lockdown measures regarding research activity have been documented as holding off all non-COVID-19 related research activities.

The postponement or cancellation of nearly all conferences has occurred at both national and international levels. Moreover, each research institute has had to make their own decision as to whether to continue research activities (ensuring all safety measures are put in place) or to shut down completely (Nassisi et al., 2020).

On the other hand, the pandemic has also stimulated new opportunities in research. In response to the challenges posed, governments and other agencies around the world have provided funding for research into COVID-19 itself and many research institutions have responded by rearranging their research topics to prioritize COVID-19-related research activities. Another opportunity that individual researchers and groups have seized during lockdown and social distancing is to publish outstanding material, as well as publish COVID-19-related research in a very short time frame. This has been encouraged since the outbreak of the pandemic with the speeding up of the publication process and special issues of journals (particularly online first) relating to the impact of the pandemic. Indeed, some academic journals have minimized the publication process duration by 49%, resulting in an average 57 days from initial submission to publication. Others have achieved an 80% time decrease in comparison to the pre-crisis situation, with an average of 14 days. In addition to the acceleration of the publication process, the number of papers submitted and published has also increased substantially (Horbach, Serge 2020).

One of the main research topics since the emergence of the COVID pandemic surrounds the infection fatality rate (IFR). IFR is considered as an estimate of the overall mortality from COVID-19 as judged by medical experts and epidemiologists (Meyerowitz-Katz & Merone 2020). Experts have reported that IFR differs completely from the case fatality rate, which is defined as an estimate of the number of deaths in relation to the total number of cases (Giorgi Rossi et al., 2020).

The study of the prevalence and severity of COVID-19 is emerging as one of the areas that epidemiologists are looking at, as study of prevalence and severity is of vital importance to compare the severity between patients with chronic diseases, especially immunity-related diseases as diabetes or hypertension. This type of study could provide good guidance for the prevention and potential treatment of COVID-19 infection (Hu et al., 2020).

Another area brought on by the crisis is research into virology studies. The study of the viral genome structure, characterizing the COVID-19 genome structure and the main differences in its structure from those studied previously may play a pivotal role in understanding the infectious capability, the pathogenesis of the diseases resulted and the differentiation mechanism (Wu et al., 2020; Zhang et al., 2020). Immunopathology and the human immune reaction toward virus infection are also of interest to researchers. The human immune response plays a key role in the control and resolution of CoV infections and decides the clinical outcome of infection. The inflammatory response and cytokines flare-up associated with infection, and their role in the pathogenesis of the disease, are the basics of therapeutic intervention trials. This type of research is one of the top fields of published papers during the pandemic (Guo et al., 2020).

The COVID-19 pandemic has led to an overwhelming universal health crisis leading to large-scale behavioural and psychological changes. Consequently, social science research topics relevant to pandemics have evolved, including work on clarifying threats, social and cultural influences, and crisis-related behaviour. Moreover, communication science, decision-making, leadership, and stress and coping are new emerging subjects to be discussed and studied (Bavel et al., 2020). Educational institutions have been closed to suppress the spread of COVID-19 pandemic (Zhu& Liu 2020), which led to challenges to the educational systems and their stakeholders. Problems included preparing their institution to adapt to the crisis within a short timeframe, reconstructing curricula, redesigning assessment plans, and preparing their staff for remote teaching in a digital and virtual manner. Universities also have the responsibility of reassuring all students, including research students, about the impact of the pandemic on their studies and research projects (Daniel 2020).

Much research has also evolved to discuss the positive impact of COVID-19 pandemic on education and how universities can benefit and recover from this experience. These valuable education-based studies have concluded that the outbreak resulted in acceleration of the development of online learning at all levels of education, even in primary schools. All types of technologies were utilized to help both online and virtual learning process including use of the internet, databases, and artificial intelligence. A shift from the traditional teacher-centred method of teaching towards a more student-centred approach has been implemented, which is a positive way forward. Assessments measuring students' teamwork activities, discussions, and conducting mini-projects have been found to be very successful methods of assessing student's work. Utilising untraditional digital teaching and learning materials as well as virtual interaction should be considered a new strategic plan for learning (Jandrić et al. 2018; Zhu& Liu 2020).

BOX 5.1   CASE STUDY: FINAL YEAR PHD STUDENT

I am a PhD student, originally from Saudi Arabia but now living with my three children here in the UK. Holding a PhD degree from one of the UK best universities was one of my life objectives. I worked hard for this dream. Today, I consider myself as a lucky person for being a student here. The times I spent here since I came in July 2016, was full of incredibly personal and academical development for myself as an international student and for my three children. We learned by a new way of education that promoted research and self-learning. We made a lot of friends from different cultures; we learned new healthy habits and skills. Honestly, I hoped that my beautiful days could last longer. At the same time, I was trying to keep myself occupied to avoid the sadness of departing by making future plans for the last months for me and my family in the UK after I get the degree; which places I should visit before I go back home to Saudi Arabia? What type of shopping to do? How am I going to say goodbye to my neighbours, my friends, my professors? How are my children going to cope with their new schools and the new education system in Saudi Arabia? I was sailing peacefully in my boat, and I didn't expect any storms, like anyone else.

After the announcement of the first case of COVID-19 in my city in March 2020, everything went fast. I did not have a lot of choice, either to stay alone with my three children at home or to leave to Saudi Arabia. The Saudi government had opened registration for evacuation flights to Saudi Arabia for five days only. I preferred the first choice, especially because my thesis submission date was soon (September 2020). I should work day and night to submit the first draft. But how? I was experiencing great stress. I was thinking of my children all the times, what could happen to them if anything happened to me? We do not have any family members in the UK, although there was a wonderful community supporting a group of people who volunteer to do shopping or taking pets for a walk. But not to stay with COVID-19 cases. Who would volunteer to stay with my children at home if I had to stay at the hospital for a while (if that happened)? Definitely, no one.

I was lost; what should I do? I wrote an email to my supervisors because I was so desperate, and I described my critical situation. It took less than 30 minutes and I received very warm and supportive emails from all my supervisory team telling me that they will always be there to help me when I ask for help. They told me to do what I think is the best for me and for my family. That was all that I need to take the decision. I am very grateful for my supportive supervisors.

I returned to Saudi Arabia. The experience was weird. I could not expect to see the Heathrow airport almost empty of travellers, that was so sad and scary. The pandemic had really changed the world. I spent the next two weeks in quarantine with my children in a hotel. Saudi Arabia was under complete lockdown when we arrived, the situation was depressing. I did not find any source of motivation, or any incentive to keep me working on the thesis. Again I discussed my worries with my supervisor, she was so cooperative as always, and again, she supported my second decision, which was to extend the submission date for six months. I had to take this decision because of the pandemic and my supervisor accepted and supported this choice. Finally, I began feeling a little bit more relaxed. Also, the staff at the postgraduate office made my situation so much less stressful. They supported and finalized my submission extension within two days.

Today, we still live under a lot of precautional regulations and restrictions because of the COVID-19 pandemic, but I feel much better than before. I am working daily on my thesis with high enthusiasm. I thank my university and my very supportive supervisors for helping me to overcome this critical situation.

Researchers: Stay Safe, Creative, and Productive

The challenge of rapidly implementing solutions to fight COVID-19 has presented logistic, financial, and political obstacles that require collaboration between governmental and private agencies (Omary et al., 2020). The COVID-19 pandemic has also affected research centres and fields.

Researchers, especially the most junior, may have felt frustrated during the pandemic as they have been unable to conduct their ongoing research activities, due to campuses being closed and individuals being locked down by governmental regulations and laws. So, working remotely has been the only solution to such a problem. Numerous virtual communication tools have been utilized. Although these have not been as effective as face-to-face communication in some ways, various methods have allowed researchers to maintain contact with their research activities, including writing grants, collecting and analysing data via electronic questionnaires, retrospective studies, writing review articles or submitting completed manuscripts for publication (Omary et al., 2020). Researchers have also been arranging regular virtual meetings and webinars.

Online meetings with laboratory colleagues and assistants can be carried out as well as scientific discussions and journal clubs (University of Michigan Medical School Office of Research 2020; Conte &Omary2018). An important upcoming opportunity for junior researchers is COVID-19-related research, for example research into biomedical, social, psychological and education-related aspects of the pandemic (Omary et al., 2020).

Cancelled Conferences

The second main challenge is how researchers can progress to gather and/or generate the required knowledge during this transitory but extended interval of social distancing, particularly research that requires physical interaction with stakeholders (Spurlock 2020). Conferences and scientific meetings have been cancelled by conference societies all over the world in response to the pandemic situation. Those conferences which were not cancelled at the start of the emergency showed much lower attendance due to many factors, such as researchers cancelling travel either voluntarily or due to governmental regulations (Robins, 2020; Service, 2020). These difficult decisions were taken in order to support the global public protection measures.

These conference cancellation measures could have negative impacts affecting the scientific research community as researchers consider conferences and other forms of scientific meetings as an investment in their career. Conferences provide many with the opportunity to gain more knowledge and receive direct feedback on their own work. Moreover, conferences provide an excellent opportunity to get to know peers, colleagues, and potential collaborators in the same fields all over the world.

A list of recommendations was postulated by Weissgerber et al (2020) to alleviate the negative impacts of conference cancellations on researchers. The conference committee should consider the financial burden of the researcher and facilitate cost reimbursement, as researchers of low-income countries have limited funding. Even though they tend to be the lowest-paid, often the costs of attending these scientific meetings is out of their own pocket (Malloy, 2020). So, reimbursement of researchers for cancelled transportation and registration fees is vital or to move the funding to the next event (Hines, 2020) with institutions covering the remaining costs to mitigate financial overload. Early-career researchers (ECRs) may be one group more affected by conference cancellations, so they may also be focused on for reimbursement measures.

Another method to alleviate cancellations that has been employed during the pandemic is moving conferences to a virtual experience (McKimm et al 2020). These are an alternative to cancelling and can be live-streamed to allow remote participation. Virtual conferences provide many benefits, such as reducing the need to travel, being cheaper to organize, and so on. When organisations are struggling with the financial impact of the pandemic, then saving money through shifting to virtual meetings might prove to be taken forward into the future. Online networking events can also be facilitated to provide opportunities for workshops and, interviews can also be held virtually for positions needed for graduates and postdoctoral researchers or for general jobs. Finally, the scientific community should ensure that cancelled talks and papers are recorded as 'accepted' for presentation on the researchers' CVs (Weissgerber et al., 2020).

BOX 5.3   KAU'S RESEARCH ACTIVITIES DURING COVID-19 PANDEMIC

In March 2020 King Abdulaziz University announced the university president's initiative reward for outstanding COVID-19 research work. Two hundred and thirty proposals were submitted in different areas. Forty two proposals fulfilled the requirements and won their competition. The research committees focused on proposals that provided creative solutions and supported community participation in areas including medical, social, economic, infrastructure, technology, and environmental fields. The initiative was launched to encourage and motivate researchers to conduct distinguished studies to deal with this pandemic, provide a view to scientific prediction of what can happen in the short and long term, analyse the available data, review theses, publications and scientific articles of the pandemic, develop fast and effective methods for diagnosing the disease, work to develop treatment options to confront the global epidemic and limit its spread, and propose solutions to the economic and social problems of the virus. In the same line, KAU published several articles dealing with COVID-19 from different points of view including medical, educational and social aspects. A team from KAU, Jazan University, Umm Al-Qura University, Imam Mohammed Ibn Saud Islamic University and Al-Faisal University published a narrative review on the therapeutic use of chloroquine and hydroxychloroquine in COVID-19 and other viral infections (Hashem et al., 2020).

Another research describing The King Abdulaziz University (KAU) Pandemic Framework, to Leverage Social Media for the Sustainable Management of Higher Education in Crisis, was published in Sustainability journal (AI-Youbi et al., 2020). A unique Online Learning Portfolio (COVID-19 OLP) for Monitoring Online Learning During COVID-19 Pandemic was developed by a team in college of Medicine and Pharmacy in KAU (Alrefaie, Hassanien and Al-Hayani, 2020). A unique research perspective on developing a Model for Utilizing Distance Learning post COVID-19 using (PACT)™ , through cross sectional qualitative study, was submitted to BMC Medical Education (Ahmed et al., no date). Another cross sectional study to evaluate Knowledge, Attitude and Practice Toward COVID-19 Among the Public in the Kingdom of Saudi Arabia, was published in Frontiers in Public Health (Al-Hanawi et al., 2020). The Emerging Faculty Needs for Enhancing Student Engagement on a Virtual Platform was studied by a team from KAU, ASU-MENA-FRI (the FAIMER regional institute in Ain Shams University Faculty of Medicine) and Arabian Gulf university and published in MedEdPublish (Ahmed, Shehata and Hassanien, 2020).

Many researchers are now in their final steps or even in the stage of writing the results and discussion of their manuscripts and will be published soon with the affiliation of KAU.

International Students and Scholarships

The COVID-19 pandemic affects all aspects of higher education, from an undergraduate and postgraduate level, including international students with scholarships. Many obstacles, economic and financial, have been encountered by international students (Hope 2020). The pandemic has presented them with important time-dependent decisions about whether to return to their home countries or to stay until the crisis passed. Universities and research centres worked assiduously to assist international students to return home and established means of enabling them to complete their academic programmes online amid the COVID-19 pandemic. This required close collaboration with the providers of education abroad programmes and international university partners. Many research and study institutions decided to adapt to the upcoming academic year standards to provide alternative education for the large number of the international students whose academic-year education abroad programmes were discontinued.

Some opportunities and ideas that have been considered for international students and scholarships in response to the COVID-19 pandemic are described below (Whalen 2020). These include online learning and virtual education abroad, domestic study away, faculty-led programming, and global education.

- Online learning and virtual education abroad: Online learning platforms provide tools to deliver course contents, programme guides, and assessment plans as well as to connect students to organisations before they start new programmes. Online platforms have become more important for organisations to help their students return back to learning and aid progression in their research projects. Education abroad programmes have even offered virtual internships. Through these, students in the United States (for example) can complete an internship with an organization located abroad. These experiences can expand and facilitate education abroad when other means are not available. While virtual education abroad will never be a substitute for direct study, it may be used in a blended manner during a crisis situation.

- Domestic study away: Many institutions (e.g. in the United States) offer domestic study-away experiences, which serve to fulfil goals similar to those traditionally associated with education abroad, as the COVID-19 pandemic means all places outside homes equally carry risk, even domestic campuses. This can fulfil the goals traditionally associated with education abroad.

- Faculty-led programming: International students who have returned home to overseas face challenges when working with faculty program leaders to continue the process of education abroad. Potential innovations in unique situations like this are needed and can be based on cultural resources and perspectives. These ideas involve cross-border collaborations and a more universal approach to disciplines. The pandemic has encouraged faculty to think about a universal approach that results in education abroad becoming established into the courses that are offered on campuses, but in novel innovative ways.

- Global education: The lockdown and associated reduction in global travel, and consequently education abroad, has reminded researchers, international students and education organizations of the adverse environmental footprints that travellers leave. Each education abroad programme should deal with the crisis sequelae considering how they can be environmentally responsible in a co-ordinated and inter-related world. It is also mandatory to involve and support education abroad students, faculty members, and administrators to offset their environmental footprints. Many educations abroad programmes and stakeholders and providers have created and developed effective methods for doing this.

Conclusions and Recommendations

The COVID-19 pandemic and subsequent forced lockdown affected research all over the world, at many levels. Research directly related to COVID-19 rapidly proliferated over those not related to COVID-19, with the appearance of new areas of research into infection fatality rates, viral immunopathology, and COVID-19 induced psychological effects. For individual researchers, remote working and virtual communication became the only available options during social distancing and forced lockdown. This meant research, conferences and scientific meetings had to be abandoned or postponed, if they could not be carried out virtually. International students and those on scholarships also encountered many challenges during the COVID-19 pandemic-related lockdown. These challenges included economic obstacles, prohibited physical interaction with their stakeholders, and reduced progress on their research, particularly if this was time-dependent and limited by the permitted duration of their scholarships. Finally, in Box 5.4, we make some recommendations to help those engaged with or planning research overcome some of the challenges that have emerged as a result of this pandemic.

BOX 5.4   RECOMMENDATIONS FOR RESEARCHERS

1   Universities and research teams need to develop and implement crisis management plans, with many Plan Bs or even Plan Cs, to be able to respond and adapt to any crisis situations or emergencies that might have a negative impact on research activities.

2   Flexibility in research topics and areas is essential as research topics will need to be rearranged and prioritized according to the world's requirements and societal needs. Having such flexibility will help in solving any emerging health-related or other world problems.

3   Accelerating the development and encouraging the use of online learning community tools and virtual platforms is vital at all educational levels utilising both teacher-centred and student-centred methods of teaching and learning. All of these measures should be considered to adapt to any possible forced lockdown, social distancing or other situations.

4   Researchers should adapt to any logistic, financial, or political obstacles that may hinder their research activity and progress.

5   Virtual interactions, meetings, and webinars should be implemented more widely to provide alternatives to conference cancellation or interference with travelling and physical interaction.

6   Many alternative opportunities and ideas should be considered for international students and scholarships to prevent any possible hindrance to their progress. These include online learning and virtual education abroad, domestic study away, faculty-led programmes, and global education.

Chapter 6

Leadership Through Crisis, Change and Uncertainty

Professor Judy McKimm
Associate Professor Paul Kneath Jones

The COVID-19 pandemic has caused huge change and uncertainty for universities and their stakeholders around the world. For many universities, the pandemic has caused an unforeseen crisis, the ripples from which will probably be felt for years to come.

Drawing from a range of literature and the authors' experience, this chapter will consider issues for organisations, programmes and individuals involved in responding to the issues raised by the pandemic, and provide guidance for managing change, uncertainty and crisis. We will describe some change approaches and models (from relatively simple, 'linear' approaches to those more appropriate for change in complex systems). Box 1 lists twelve useful tips (McKimm and Jones, 2018) which, whilst described in the context of curriculum design and delivery, can be adapted to a range of change situations and contexts. We will use some of these tips and apply them to the COVID-19 pandemic and its impact on universities.

1. Identify the purpose and scope of change
2. Create the vision, aligned to mission
3. Develop a strategy for change involving key stakeholders
4. Quick visible wins and communication are vital
5. Analyse the internal environment and culture
6. Consider the external environment, cultural contexts and political influences
7. Choose the right combination of approaches to change
8. Use project management techniques for operational planning and implementation
9. Acknowledge the psychological impact of change
10. Plan for transition and loss of competence
11. Don't underestimate the complexity
12. Celebrate success and the shift from project to 'new reality'

(McKimm and Jones, 2018)

Some Definitions

In this chapter we are focusing on leadership and change, so some definitions are helpful. We conceptualise 'leadership' as comprising three interrelated elements: leadership, management and followership (see Figure 6.1), which we call the *leadership triad* (McKimm and O'Sullivan 2016).

The "Leadership triad"
(McKimm and O'Sullivan 2016)

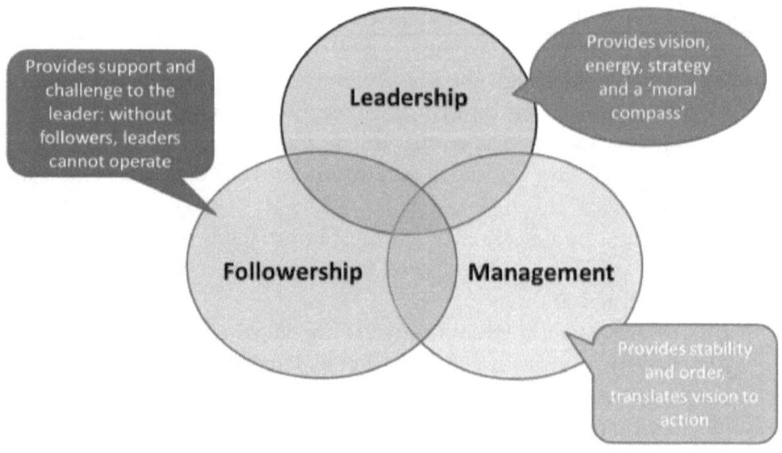

FIGURE 6.1 THE LEADERSHIP TRIAD

As you can see in Figure 6.1, leadership tends to be about movement and change, and leadership puts the power and energy into a system or initiative, whereas management of systems, processes and policies enables the enactment of the leadership vision or goals and helps make change happen. Followership provides the leadership with the 'people power' to enact the change. Without active followers, leadership cannot happen, as leaders cannot do everything themselves. Even the most senior of leaders do not 'lead' all the time—in 'real life' we move around these three elements as we lead, manage and follow in various situations.

Responding to Crisis and Planning Change

University leadership has been hugely tested during the pandemic crisis which is very different from leading in 'normal' times. A crisis is any event that is going (or is expected) to lead to an unstable, difficult and/or dangerous situation affecting an individual, group, community, or whole society. In times of crisis and uncertainty, difficult, important decisions must be made amidst a lack of information about the future. In the middle of a crisis everything can look like impossible to overcome, or as if things are failing. Any crisis is experienced at organisational and team levels, and with the pandemic it has also impacted on individual students and faculty and, for many, their normal coping mechanisms may be insufficient.

BOX 6.2   COMMENTARY: AN EDUCATIONAL LEADERSHIP CRISIS – PROFESSOR SHERIF ELASAADANY

One of the first things university leaders must recognize is that universities are facing a crisis. According to Garcia (2006), when leaders see a crisis slowly developing, they need to overcome normalcy bias, which can lead them to undervalue the crisis and its possible impacts. Furthermore, once a crisis is recognized, leaders can begin to mount a response, which will be different from a response in a routine emergency, and therefore they need to follow the plans drawn up in advance (McKinsey & Company, 2020). Unfamiliarity and uncertainty dominate a crisis; therefore, effective responses are largely improvised. Leaders may not only take temporary actions like endorsement of online teaching policies, but they may take other actions such as making new adjustments to ongoing practices or adopting new tools that can be maintained even after the crisis passes. During the crisis, a predetermined response plan is not needed, but rather behaviours and mindsets to deal with the situation need to be developed, without overreaction to previous developments. Above all, people must keep looking forward.

A task force should be set up after consultations with all key stakeholders. This should be done in a timely manner to speed up the process of handling subsequent issues and problems. Ensuring continuity requires policy adjustments, and a dedicated communication link must be in place to facilitate direct communication. This aims at getting feedback and making the required changes. One of the key lessons in crisis decision-making is that being quick in decision-making on policy adjustments should be supplemented by listening to those who are most affected by these decisions. Another key issue is the need to conduct surveys to monitor how far the strategies, policies and procedures are affected.

Good leadership requires key characteristics such as:

- Honesty and confidence that continuity of business is what matters
- Being decisive but adaptable as feedback is received
- Exercising caution and reason when making decisions
- Controlling potential chaos
- Staying positive all the time.

University leaders need to orient staff members to make the necessary decisions that affect students and international students. They have to suggest alternative teaching methods, including ICT (information and computer-based technologies)-mediated learning. The faculty in general and ICT staff in particular need to make sure that the ICT infrastructure can deal efficiently with the immediate migration to the online methodology. As traditional universities move to online learning, we need to remember that this is a temporary solution. Effective online teaching cannot happen overnight, as it requires mobilization of time, effort and training. The skill of teaching online is not an instantly transferable skill, and it is important to remember that the universities that excel in online teaching put in a lot of time and effort to be recognized as such.

It is however possible to come out of crisis stronger than before if leaders operate with a 'people first culture' and pay 'attention to three things: establishing clear accountability in the leadership ranks; developing a nuts-and-bolts, collaborative plan for getting through the crisis; and putting a separate group in charge of defining the "new normal," when the worst is over' (Kantor, 2020). As the pandemic elapsed around the world, leaders needed to also be highly adaptive and flexible, adjusting their outcomes and approaches based on rapidly changing information.

Adaptive leadership (Heifetz et al 2009; Randall & Coakley 2007) is a good approach when responding to change, uncertainty and crisis, not in a technical way (by simply applying familiar processes and ways of working) but by involving people throughout the organisation to help solve *wicked* problems.

'Wicked' problems do not have clear solutions and, in times of uncertainty, new ways of working may be required. Adaptive leaders create the organisational conditions that enable dynamic networks and environments to achieve identified goals in such uncertainty. Adaptive leadership focuses on four dimensions: navigating organisational/system environments; leading with empathy; learning through self-correction and reflection; and creating win-win solutions.

One of the most useful concepts in adaptive leadership which helps leaders to make decisions is being able to diagnose the *'precious'* from the *'expendable'*. What do we mean by this? The *'precious'* is what is vitally important to the organisation, in education this is the learners themselves, the faculty, and the quality of educational provision - you don't want to lose the focus on these as you respond to crisis and change. What is *'expendable'*? Curiously, because of campus closures due to the pandemic, suddenly the large lecture theatres, shiny new buildings and campuses that many universities see as artefacts of success, actually become expendable. Once the *'new normal'* occurs, we will no doubt see a return to campuses and utilisation of buildings again, but adaptive leaders recognise what is precious and make sure that this is looked after and nurtured. We must remember this once the crisis is past and nurture the people and the values that make higher education special.

We can see that across the world, universities (many of which had never provided online learning or assessment) suddenly had to decide how (or whether) they would (or could) provide educational opportunities for their students. Cameron and Green (2015) suggest that leaders responding to or stimulating change need to balance their efforts across three dimensions of any change: *outcomes, interests and emotions*.

In terms of *'outcomes'*, they stress that clear outcomes (deliverables) must be developed and implemented. Outcomes (goals, targets or objectives) need to be SMART (specific, measurable, achievable, realistic and timebound). In times of immediate crisis, some goals will need to be very short-term (e.g. *'ensure all faculty are able and prepared to work from home by the end of next week'*), whereas strategically, senior leaders have the responsibility to keep the longer terms outcomes in mind (e.g. *'ensure that the university remains financially viable'*). The role of the leader is to enable people and the culture to adapt to the change by working with and acknowledging their emotions (Cameron and Green 2015). Leaders also need to pay attention to (what may be competing) *interests*, here they need to mobilize their influence, authority and power to enact the change.

Project management techniques are helpful for operational planning and implementation. During the pandemic, plans will need to be devised and aligned in a range of areas (learning and teaching, student and faculty wellbeing, research, estates, finance etc.) and at many levels: whole university, department, programme and course. A project management approach sees activities as temporary, non-routine, acknowledging uncertainty and with a defined end point. Many project planning and management approaches exist, and for large projects, software such as Microsoft Project™ can be helpful. A project plan should include the following: key actions and deliverables; who is accountable and responsible for what; timeframe/schedule; financial breakdown and budgets; resources; risk mitigation; stakeholder engagement plan and communication strategy (Gardner 2017). Tools such as GANTT charts, critical path analysis, options appraisal, risk and stakeholder analysis and communication strategies are all readily available online (e.g., JISC 2017).

Techniques taking a *'linear'* view of change such as Lewin's *'freeze/unfreeze'* model (Lewin 1951; Cummings et al. 2016) can be useful in framing the response into simple terms rather than getting bogged down in complexity. These look at the change process as comprising three steps: current state (how the university and programmes ran pre-pandemic); transitional state (how the university runs during the pandemic); desired state (how might the university run after the pandemic, in the *'new normal'*). Once the broad elements and strategy has been agreed, then the detailed planning and implementation stages begin.

Risk Analysis

In an ideal world, all changes would be able to be planned for and there would be no surprises. However, successful organisations (and individuals) do actually plan for unforeseen circumstances in order to stay resilient and help mitigate risk. There are a number of ways of assessing risks, with one of the most widely used being a 'risk matrix' (Figure 6.2). This is used during risk assessment to define the level of risk by considering the category of probability or likelihood against the category of consequence severity. This simple tool helps to increase the visibility of risks and assist management decision making. At the university level as well as departmental and programme levels, a risk analysis should be carried out and updated regularly. In stable times, this helps the organisation keep aware of external and internal risk factors and to put plans in place, and during the pandemic identifying and working out how to overcome the dangers becomes much more vital.

Example Risk Matrix

Likelihood	Consequences				
	Insignificant *Risk is easily mitigated by normal day to day processes*	**Minor** *Some extra costs, delays or loss of income*	**Moderate** *Significant costs, loss of income or reputational damage*	**Major** *Severe impact on organisation/ programme*	**Catastrophic** *The organisation (or large parts of it) may not survive*
Certain (>90% chance)	HIGH	HIGH	EXTREME	EXTREME	EXTREME
Likely (50-90% chance)	MODERATE	HIGH	HIGH	EXTREME	EXTREME
Moderate (50-90% chance)	LOW	MODERATE	HIGH	EXTREME	EXTREME
Unlikely (3-10% chance)	LOW	LOW	MODERATE	HIGH	EXTREME
Rare <3% chance	LOW	LOW	MODERATE	HIGH	HIGH

FIGURE 6.2 RISK ANALYSIS MATRIX

Plan for a transitional stage

Even in this time of crisis, which has happened so quickly, universities and programmes are still moving from an 'old' to a 'new' way of working and the transition must be planned in practical terms. Specific questions to be asked include:

- Are we making changes permanently or are they going to be short-lived and only relevant while the crisis is ongoing?
- What do we do about students who have missed essential elements of their programme?

It is of paramount importance to consider the 'ripple effect' of making decisions in an uncoordinated way, which can lead to unintended consequences. For example, if we decide not to run final examinations for one year group, weak students may progress to the next year when really they should have failed. So, how do we address that?

The fundamental shift to an online eLearning format is a major transformational change which will arise from many conversations and planning decisions. It demands a shift in educational philosophies (e.g., towards a more learner-centred approach) and also changes to common routine practices (e.g., loss of face-to-face lectures). Lewin's 'forcefield analysis' (1947) helps us to consider the drivers and resistors (pushing for and against the change). A key driver is the pandemic but we must (as Lewin suggests) work with the resistors, listening and talking with people to understand what their issues are and overcome the challenges we face.

Develop a strategy for change and communication involving key stakeholders

The creation of a *guiding coalition* (Kotter, 1996) is essential to enable stakeholders (in this case, administrators, leader, faculty and students) to work collaboratively to manage the new ways of working. It is essential that senior leaders are involved (Mintzberg, 1987) so that resources can be mobilised at pace when necessary, as they are often gatekeepers of resources (e.g., finances, people, IT systems).

Kotter suggests that change leaders need to establish and communicate a 'sense of urgency' as a key driver for change (1996). In the situation of the pandemic, however, the sense of urgency was an external driver which required universities and teachers to respond quickly. Leaders needed a good understanding of organisational resources, the external environment and educational responses worldwide to develop meaningful and realistic strategies (Schwartzstein et al. 2008).
A formal communications strategy is required which provides consistent messages and opportunities for questions to be answered for all key stakeholders. Kotter also suggests the generation of and communication about 'quick visible wins', such as learners returning to their studies or a successfully run online assessment, will help maintain motivation.

The development of a response strategy must take into account both the internal and external environment. Any planned changes to combat the challenges of the crisis need to take into consideration the IT resources, skills mix of staff and the funding of any new innovations. Analysis of the environment can be done in a number of ways. For example, a simple but effective *SWOT* analysis can encourage you to think about what strengths your team (or organisation as a whole) already has while highlighting the weaknesses and most importantly the threats to the education of students. Another tool is McKinseys *7S* model (Peters and Waterman, 1982) which is an integrated way of approaching change. This model reminds us that changing any one of the seven elements of the model (staff, skills, style, strategy, system, structure and superordinate goals/values) will have an impact on all the others.

Having a team (the guiding coalition) to think about these areas will highlight what needs to go into a strategy to overcome problems before they arise. The superordinate goals or values at the centre of this model are what the organisation stands for: its central beliefs, attitudes and core values. This is important when considering strategy, as one of the tenets of various Middle Eastern countries has previously been that distance and online learning is not an acceptable means of providing higher education. Therefore the strategy must acknowledge central beliefs in its plans as this requires major policy and culture shifts.

Rather than overly considering the internal concepts, Mintzberg and Lampel (1998) suggest organisations should concentrate on the external concerns. It is vital that when such major changes are being made, thought is given to the external regulatory bodies in a country which may demand different requirements of programmes (particularly professional programmes). Changing the way in which a programme is essentially taught (the move to an online learning format) may well have implications on the recruitment of future students which is a major financial consideration. A useful tool to consider all the elements of the external environment is the PESTLE (PEST or PESTELI) model, see Figure 6.3. This model enables the stakeholders to analyse the effect of the changes from six different perspectives.

PESTLE model

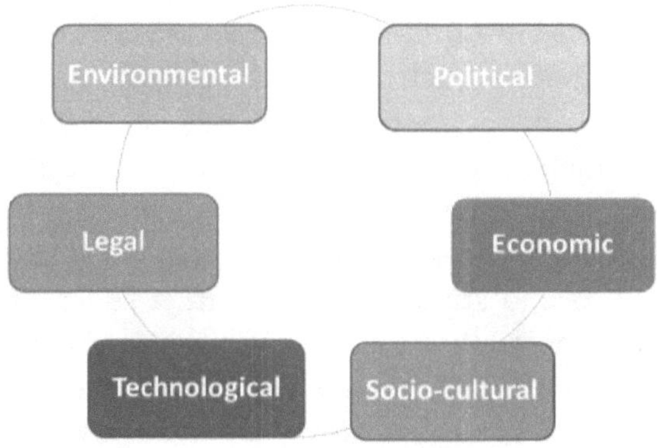

FIGURE 6.3 PESTLE MODEL.

Choose the right combination of approaches to change

Being able to utilise different approaches to your style of leadership and change management is important in being able to adapt to the crisis. A straightforward change (such as requiring faculty to work from home) needs a more directive approach whereas a more complex situation within uncertainty requires the leader to facilitate the conditions for emergent change: change that emerges out of conversations and responses to a situation. For example, planning the return to campus for staff and students will require a series of various plans to deal with an uncertain situation. Whilst working through change and transition, the effects on various learner cohorts must be carefully planned to avoid groups missing essential elements of a programme which could lead to potentially poor downstream consequences. People resist change for many reasons (Kotter and Schlesinger, 1979). All change involves a loss of something to all stakeholders, and educators must work empathically, drawing on their emotional intelligence (Goleman, 1995) to ensure they listen to their students and teams so as to enthuse, motivate and encourage them to engage with the changes that have been imposed upon them.

Just as change brings about a loss, it also produces a drop in initial competence. Bridges' (2004) three zone transition model describes this in terms of ending, losing and letting go. In this crisis it is important to work people to help them cope with these new ways of working. Individuals cope with change differently (Kralik et al, 2006). For example, some members of your team will become *'early adopters'* (Rogers, 2003) of online learning and volunteer readily for the challenges ahead, whereas the 'laggards' will struggle to adapt to not having face-to-face teaching. Through listening, you, as a leader, can encourage them to adapt and one way of enabling this is to *'empower broad based action'* (Kotter, 1996) by giving individuals clear roles and aspects of the plan to deal with. This encourages engagement and makes people feel part of the team, which is especially important when people are working remotely.

Working in a complex environment brings challenges. In a complex system, such as a university, people have the freedom to act (agency) in ways that are not always predictable (Kernick and Swanwick, 2007) and in crisis leaders need to fully understand and explain the changes being made and utilise a range of measures to make this happen. In complex, uncertain environments, people have to be able to work in ambiguity, adopt a systems' thinking approach, connect people up with one other and make the vision for the change easy to understand (Thornton, 2013). A useful model to help us understand the approach and impact of change is Stacey's (2001) *certainty agreement matrix*. The model describes the four zones of simple, complicated, complex and chaotic. This model explains that the further we are from either agreement or certainty, the more likely we are to be working in a complex zone. In order to make changes happen we need to provide some certainty and help people to reach agreement on the course of action to be taken, so we move into the *'simple'* zone. An example of this is that when the pandemic hit our countries, many countries and regions moved into lockdown, with restricted movements. Universities responded to this potential chaos and complexity by providing agreement about what would happen, even if there was uncertainty about timings and the course of the pandemic. So faculty were required to work from home and students also returned home, many back to their home countries, campuses were closed, new policies were established and online learning was established. This enabled people to carry on with their studies and work, even if there was much uncertainty about the external environment.

Conclusions

This chapter, structured round the *'12 tips'*, provides different strategies, models and frameworks within which educators, managers and administrators can utilise change models to work with and manage the impact and consequences arising from the pandemic more effectively and efficiently. Whilst we have not encountered such a global crisis before, by working collaboratively and acknowledging the complexity of the changes, we can help maintain continuity of university activities and support all those who work and learn within universities. Sharing practice and learning from others who have successfully implemented changes in this crisis, through attending or running seminars or webinars and publishing papers, is an excellent way of celebrating what you have achieved. As the pandemic runs its course, universities will need to decide whether the changes they implemented to combat this crisis are permanent and become *'the way we do things around here'* (Bower, 1996) or whether they are merely transitional arrangements until the crisis is over.

Chapter 7

Looking forward: Perspectives on the longer-term impact of the pandemic on universities

Professor Judy McKimm

Chloe Mills

Professor Abdulrahman O Al-Youbi

It is easy for us to sit here and write, reflecting on the impacts of the pandemic or what positivity we can draw from it, and forget the real pain that people have felt worldwide during this global crisis. At the time of writing (27 July 2020), there are over 16.2 million cases of COVID-19 in 188 countries or regions, and the global pandemic has claimed over 649,000 lives (Johns Hopkins). Cases are still rising around the world, and whilst hopes for an effective vaccine are high, it remains unclear when or whether this will actually be available.

It is this grief and loss, combined with not knowing what will happen in the future, that underpins the insecurity felt by universities at this moment. This uncertainty poses great problems for universities and for current and potential students when considering how and when to return to campus. The university's and teachers' capacity and concerns need to be balanced with students' needs and concerns.

From a student perspective, they will have challenges and worries about their programme, how teaching will happen, and about their own safety and wellbeing in terms of travel and accommodation. Universities, like other organisations, have to abide by their government's laws and regulations as well as take local considerations into account. Physical distancing and other measures such as wearing face masks (or not) will play a large part in determining which programmes and students will be able to run. It is highly likely that large lecture theatres packed with students will make a return in the short term, so online streaming of live lectures and recording of lectures for students to study in their own time will become the norm. This requires a robust IT infrastructure and teachers and students to have good access to Wi-Fi at home and in social and study spaces.

Whilst teachers have become much more adept at facilitating online learning and assessment, some activities simply cannot be delivered online, such as laboratory or skills-based activities. Also, many teachers are still much more comfortable with traditional ways of teaching in lecture theatres and small discussion groups. Students have expressed concerns about the quality of their teaching when much is online and why universities are still charging high fees (especially to international students). This partly reflects the financial balancing act that universities are making - they have suffered a lot economically through the pandemic and many are very reliant on student fees as a big source of income. The more public and subsidised universities are, the lesser the financial impact. Until the new academic year begins and students enrol, it will be hard for universities to make plans based on fee income.

The toll of COVID-19 on universities can be summarised as follows:

- US – most vulnerable to loss of foreign students, but big campuses with Silicon Valley partnerships may dominate
- Australia – universities hit by COVID-19 sooner than in other parts of the world
- EU – northern states in better position than south to escape the worst
- Poland – economy has weathered coronavirus better than most, but drop in foreign demand still expected

- Ireland – the virus has infected an organism that was not 'in rude health' to begin with
- UK – crisis has exposed limitations of the high-tuition fee mode.

(Kelly, 2020)

And of course, there will be local and regional spikes of the virus, so universities may have to close down again and again, and travel restrictions and quarantining regulations may make a physical presence on campus and placements impossible. Students will want to feel physically safe, especially if they have a medical condition or live with someone who is vulnerable, and universities will need to be clear and transparent about communications and contingency plans for a range of scenarios. Accommodation will need to be reviewed to decide on whether it is safe in terms of coronavirus spread and that it meets physical distancing rules.

Universities around the world have, however, adapted rapidly to these changing circumstances. In countries where online learning was not widespread (or even discounted as a modality), now much of the teaching has been, and will continue to be, delivered online. This shift has been reflected by Ministries of Education and other agencies reviewing policies, by universities adapting their regulations and practice, and by governments providing additional funding to universities to help them adapt. Shifting to an online learning model may provide opportunities for universities to attract international students who will be able to stay in their home countries for all or a large part of their studies.

Universities have also adapted by moving semester or year start times or by adding additional entry points to programmes with the aim of attracting more students. This will place a large workload on teachers and administrators who will have to manage teaching, assessment and progression boards for multiple cohorts of learners. Depending on when campuses closed and programmes stopped or radically changed delivery mode, some student groups may need additional catch-up teaching or assessments which could increase the workload on teachers and administrators even further. This will need to be managed carefully so as not to push teachers and administrators into burnout. Other consequences of the pandemic have been on international faculty, with many scholars being unable to start new jobs or having to return to their home country.

Many commentators have postulated that the world of work will never be the same again: that remote working from home will become more commonplace, even routine; that the work day/week will be shorter or that the need for commuting and large offices will be radically reduced or even disappear.

Ravin Jesuthasan, writing on the World Economic Forum COVID Action Platform on 8 June 2020, noted that:

> *"We will need a sustainable reset of the workplace, not a short-term one. It will require a new culture and it must be dominated by two major themes: flexibility and a portfolio-based approach to work strategy … the companies that thrive will get the new work equation – flexibility plus agility plus resilience – right."*
>
> (Jesuthasan, 2020)

BOX 7.1   COMMENTS FROM A UNIVERSITY'S HIGHER ADMINISTRATION

The COVID-19 pandemic has been tough for the whole world, and every sector has been affected in one way or another; King Abdulaziz University has not been an exception, and has begun immediate contingency plans to find solutions for every aspect of the problem. The academic year 2019/2020 was a success, and the associated problems have been kept at minimum.

The most important lesson learned is that when all University departments work in harmony, any problem can be solved. Though COVID-19 posed a threat to the educational and research processes, it also created opportunities in several aspects of the university life. For example, the immediate switching to online teaching and virtual classes proves the efficacy of the University's infrastructure and ability of staff, faculty and students to adapt to new systems. However, when problems erupted due to servers' capacities to accommodate large numbers of classes at the same time, and especially classes of larger numbers of students, it took the university some time to fix the problem and find other alternatives such as introducing the new Ultra service in BlackBoard, and dividing large classes to smaller groups, among other remedial actions.

Lessons learned
-   Within the problem itself, the solution lies.
-   To confront a crisis, decision-making must be a flexible process.
-   Always prepare plan B and C.
-   When adopting a trial and error approach, remedial decisions should be swift.
-   Orientation is vital. Keep everyone aware of the threats and opportunities and update them regularly through all available means.
-   Communication is the password for success. Maintain communication with all concerned parties.
-   Know your resources and potentials and act accordingly to maximize benefits.
-   Cooperation among all sectors is a key to success.
-   Engage all parties in the process of decision making so that they feel responsible.

Looking forward
By failing to prepare, you are preparing to fail. Once another wave of the pandemic or other crises may occur, one must be well prepared. Although the University has emergency plans, we are working to develop them with a big margin of maneuverability and flexibility to redress any future misfortunate events that may occur. Alternatives are put in place for all aspects of the University work domains. For example, blended teaching approaches, research interests and quality assurance and accreditation processes are considered and revised and under further developments.

So what might this mean for universities moving forward?

The pandemic crisis has revealed that the more commercially driven universities are, especially if they have a high reliance on student fees for their survival, the more vulnerable they are. Publicly funded universities have coped better and the impact of the pandemic has been felt less. For example, as China moved into an emerging market, almost one million Chinese students are studying outside China, and the pandemic has cut right across this, compounded in some countries by governmental restrictions on visas from certain countries (Kenny, 2020).

Universities have responded in a number of ways, with some very prestigious universities such as Cambridge and Harvard deciding to run all their courses entirely online in the autumn of 2020. Other universities have taken a hybrid approach, opening campuses (or parts of them) with adherence to physical distancing models and providing all learning that can be run effectively online via that modality. Similarly, only staff members that need to return to campus will do so and others will continue to work from home. Universities are also taking great care to address cybersecurity issues as more on more of the administrative and teaching work moves online. So taking an adaptive and flexible approach will enable universities to continue to thrive.

BOX 7.2 COMMENT FROM THE STUDENT PERSPECTIVE – CHLOE MILLS

This pandemic and subsequent quarantine had made an already difficult task (doing a PhD) seem, sometimes, near impossible. An informal survey of graduate students shows that the most common problems were:

- lack of access to research materials, equipment or labs
- forced changes to research plans
- disruption to daily life
- inability to travel for fieldwork, internships, conferences, etc.
- interruptions to data collection
- not enjoying working from home
- financial hardships
- difficult living situations
- lack of focus, restlessness, general mental health issues.

This list highlights the numerous problems that have faced students during the COVID-19 crisis. If further waves hit, these problems will only recur. Students, especially graduate students, may be facing the repercussions of this global crisis for years to come.

However, to end on a more positive note, there are some silver linings. This situation has shown us the importance of community spirit, of working together, of supportive and positive working relationships, and of flexibility. Personally, my department has stepped up to support us in our research and I've found innovative ways of enhancing my CV while working from home and lockdown. I've experienced a deeper engagement with social media and have been to online conferences as well as personal development webinars and workshops hosted by my funding body. Overall, this crisis has shown how a university can exercise creative solutions and decision-making to effectively communicate with and support students in times of hardship. Looking forward, we have to remember the importance of creativity, flexibility, and working together.

The traditional concept of a university is a place where people physically meet, to debate, to learn, to collaborate on research, and to develop innovations. However, if the pandemic continues to surge around the world, and travel is restricted, the full 'traditional' campus experience may well disappear for many students in the next couple of years. However, for undergraduates in particular, the rite of passage that involves the full spectrum of university life will still be a big part of their life journey and there will still be a demand once the virus is under control. It is unclear at the time of writing whether students will choose to defer their studies until things are more settled, however, because of the impact of the pandemic on employment opportunities, studying at university (even if it is not what they hoped for) may be a more sensible option.

The pandemic has been a huge disruption for higher education institutions on an unprecedented and international scale. As we said at the start of this book, the very disruption also provides a unique opportunity for us to innovate through reflecting on what the role of universities in society is and what it could be. Making 'upstream' interventions about the nature of learning, working, studying and researching at university will allow us to make smarter decisions based on long-term thinking on these matters. A university needs to be a place that enables transformative learning to happen and promotes research and innovation. Universities also have a place in society and should thus be socially accountable. They should facilitate dialogue and exchange of views between faculty and students, and prepare students to be global citizens, ready to play their part in tackling wider social issues such as inequality and environmental sustainability. A recent international manifesto called:

> *"for mobility in higher education to be a catalyst for 'resilience and renewal' in the wake of the COVID-9 pandemic",*

suggesting that maintaining the ability for students and faculty to travel and learn from other countries, cultures and individuals is essential to ensure international collaboration and exchange.

Responding to the pandemic has produced a range of innovations, such as virtual conferences and meetings, which have enabled collaboration and conversations with much less environmental impact. Maybe these are the type of benefits that we can take forward, reflecting on the need for travel and physical meetings and moving virtually when we can, whilst still ensuring that the core activities and values that make universities such a special place to work and learn remain in place.

Finally, we conclude the book with hope for the future which no doubt will hold more challenges, not just with the pandemic but arising from the climate emergency and environmental changes, many of which are caused by human activities. Enabling universities, their students, researchers, teachers and administrators, to thrive will require strong leadership, and a commitment by all to work collaboratively to tackle these global crises: the pandemic has demonstrated how interconnected we all are, and universities are uniquely placed to take leadership and produce the global citizens we all need.

BOX 7.3   COVID-19 AND RESEARCH, LEARNED LESSONS AND STEPS FORWARD

Perhaps one of the most important lessons learned by academics and researchers in universities and research institutions during the emerging period of the COVID-19 pandemic is the importance of cooperation between different disciplines. This requires the formation of research teams that can conduct scientific research characterized by accuracy and credibility with the possibility of publishing in international journals with a high impact factor without falling into the trap of non - credibility and inaccurate data and failure to meet sound scientific standards for scientific research, including the research sample size and obtaining approvals for research and data from their original sources.

The pandemic has shown how it is easily possible for some international journals and researchers with a global reputation to make research mistakes and publish research that lacks credibility, which was discovered by the withdrawal of some research after publication in some prestigious journals. Cooperation between researchers should not be limited to research in research institutions and universities locally only, but should go beyond to global cooperation, especially in light of a pandemic threatening the entire world. This presented the need for credibility and honest cooperation between countries of the world in the exchange of information and data among them, especially in matters related to number of cases and their symptoms, the results of using different drugs in treatment, and the results of experiments and research for vaccines so that the ultimate goal is cooperation, not competition.

In addition to the lessons learned in the field of medical research, the pandemic opened a wide field for research in the field of education, sharing experiences between countries in the field of e-learning and assessment, and professional development of faculty members through the use of various techniques for holding workshops and courses and sharing successful experiences in the field of education and assessment from publishing them in the form of scientific research. A lot of research has been published in the field of education during the period of the pandemic that shows the experiences of universities and scientific institutions in the face of the impact of this pandemic on education and how to switch to e-learning in a short period of time. Scientific journals in the disciplines of education witnessed a great popularity in terms of the number of published papers, which led to a large number of them publishing special issues on education and assessment experiences during the pandemic.

The COVID-19 pandemic also showed the great differentiation between the countries of the world in the field of scientific research and the extent of the impact of what is allocated from financial resources for spending on scientific research, on the quality and speed of carrying out research in these countries compared to countries that set modest budgets for spending on scientific research.

From these lessons learned, we can proceed to the future steps that must be followed in order to face such crises in the event of their occurrence in the future through the following:

1. Continuing the work of the research work teams that were formed during the pandemic and building on the results reached and studying these results to form databases specific to this virus, which contributes to predicting its future characteristics and the extent of the possibility of genetic mutations and its return in other forms.
2. Urging all countries of the world to jointly cooperate in the field of scientific research and share the results with utmost credibility and transparency among them.
3. Increasing budgets for scientific research at the level of countries and educational and research institutions.
4. Attention to educational research and training faculty members to conduct them in correct scientific methods.
5. Spreading awareness among academics and researchers regarding the ethics of scientific research and the need to adhere to it.

Appendix 1: Checklist for an education response to the COVID-19 pandemic

1. Establish a task force or steering committee that will have responsibility to develop and implement the education response to the COVID-19 Pandemic. To the extent possible ensure those in the task force represent different constituents in the education system or school network and bring important and diverse perspectives to inform their work, for example various departments curriculum, teacher education, information technology, teacher representatives, parent representatives, students, representatives of industry when relevant.
2. Develop a schedule and means of frequent and regular communication among task force members, during the period when social distancing will be in effect.
3. Define the principles which will guide the strategy. For example: protecting the health of students and staff, ensuring academic learning and providing emotional support to students and faculty. These principles will provide focus for the initiatives to be undertaken and will help prioritize time and other limited resources.
4. Establish mechanisms of coordination with public health authorities so that education actions are in sync and help advance public health goals and strategies.
5. Re-prioritize curriculum goals.
6. Identify the feasibility of pursing options to recover learning time once the social distancing period is over.
7. Identify means of education delivery. When feasible, those should include online learning, as it provides the greatest versatility and opportunity for interaction. If not, all students have devices and connectivity, look for ways to provide them to those students. Explore partnerships with the private sector and the community in securing the resources to provide those devices and connectivity.
8. Clearly define roles and expectations for faculty to effectively steer and support students' learning in the new situation, through direct instruction where possible or guidance for self-directed learning.
9. Create a website to communicate with teachers, students and parents about curriculum goals, strategies and suggested activities and additional resources.

10. If an online education strategy is not feasible, develop alternative means of delivery, they could include TV programs, if a partnership with television stations is feasible, podcasts, radio broadcasts, and learning packets either in digital form or on paper. Explore partnerships with community organizations and the private sector to deliver those.
11. Ensure adequate support for the most vulnerable students during the implementation of the alternative education plan.
12. Enhance the communication and collaboration among students to foster mutual learning and wellbeing.
13. Create a mechanism of just in time professional development for teachers to be able to support learners in the new modality of instruction. Create modalities that foster teacher collaboration and professional communities and that increase teacher autonomy.
14. Define appropriate mechanisms of student assessment during the exigency.
15. Define appropriate mechanisms for progression and graduation.
16. As needed, revise regulatory framework in ways that make online education and other modalities feasible, and in ways that support faculty autonomy and collaboration. This includes providing school day credit for days taught in alternative education plans.
17. Each school should develop a plan for continuity of operations. As a way to support them, education authorities can provide curated examples of plans in other schools.
18. Schools should develop a system of communication with each student, and a form of checking-in daily with each student. Perhaps in the form of texts from teachers if parents have access to mobile phones.
19. Daily check-ins with staff.
20. Identify other school networks or systems and create forms of regular communications with them to share information about your needs and strategies.
21. Ensure that school leaders get the financial, logistical and moral support they need.
22. Develop a communications plan. Map key constituencies, and key messages to support the execution of the education strategy during the exigency, and ensure those are effectively communicated through various channels.

Reimers and Schleicher (2020, pp. 5-6)

Appendix 2: Case study: King Abdulaziz University's Forum activities during the COVID-19 pandemic

The King Abdulaziz University (KAU) forum of academic departments' heads and supervisors held a number of virtual meetings and lectures during the COVID-19 pandemic, as the University Vice President for Academic Affairs believes in the vital role of academic departments' heads and supervisors in the success of the educational process and scientific research, and also in overcoming different challenges at this stage. This is meant to enhance the role of the forum in informing and supporting them during the coronavirus pandemic period. As the Forum intended to support all faculty members in the Kingdom, faculty members from all Saudi universities were allowed to attend four online meetings, offering 16 lectures, streamed via Zoom™, attended by nearly 2000 faculty members.

The 5th Meeting: Distance Learning Strategies in Teaching and Testing: Confronting Coronavirus

The meeting discussed principles to be observed after reviewing the proposal of the educational strategy in the period of the pandemic. The meeting witnessed a discussion with both Professor Abdulmonem Al-Hayani, Vice President for Academic Affairs and Dr. Hisham Jameel Bardesi, Dean of E-Learning and Distance Education.

The Vice President for Academic Affairs summarized the main directives of the Ministry of Education as the proposal offered several alternatives to how to tackle the e-learning process, and discussed how to verify that the quality of outputs is not compromised in light of the existing challenges, as well as the flexible and multiple alternatives in the assessment process. The meeting made several recommendations:

1. It should be put into consideration that the regular old system cannot be entirely followed in the current period.
2. The educational process should be made easier for students through putting in place flexible mechanisms to achieve the intended learning outcomes in a creative and unconventional ways.
3. Encouraging faculty members to develop an integrated academic time plan for completing the teaching process and assessment of student performance.
4. Developing a plan to compensate students for any unachieved knowledge, skills and competencies.
5. Completing the continuous assessment using different assessment methods and tests through the university's e-learning systems, and using test alternatives to achieve educational goals and learning outcomes.
6. Supporting students in this critical period, guiding them academically, and supporting senior students to complete graduation requirements according to regulations, in a way that achieves learning outcomes.
7. Cooperation and joining efforts of all parties is needed to overcome the current crisis and challenges.

The 6th Meeting: Coronavirus and Higher Education: Global Challenges and Opportunities

The meeting discussed several aspects pertaining to university education, both for undergraduate and graduate levels. The meeting hosted Professor Judy McKimm and Associate Professor Paul Jones, and also examined possible solutions for supervision of PhD theses and research from Saudi and international perspectives. The two scholars discussed what a teacher and the University might need to overcome the crisis from the educational perspective. The recommendations of the meeting included:

1. Keeping students and faculty safe & supported.
2. Maintaining communication.

3. Maintaining continuity of teaching/learning.
4. Continuation of research (especially when people are involved) and supervision.
5. Longer term considerations, such as quality assurance and recruitment.

The 7th Meeting: Brainstorming on Developing Distance Learning and Assessment

In appreciation of the vital role of faculty members and academic departments' heads and supervisors in rendering the e-learning process a success and overcoming the current challenges, the forum held the 7th meeting in 1441 AH. The meeting aimed to engage in discussions and benefit from their ideas in putting in place a policy that meet the needs of the current stage and guarantee the continuity of the educational process. After discussions and SWOT analysis, the meeting made the following recommendations:

1. Developing clear regulations, laws and policies for marks distribution and assessment processes, which outline mechanisms for filing complaints, grievances and receiving student suggestions.
2. Preparing an excelled interactive content for curricula, theoretical and practical lessons and assessments to reduce cheating and plagiarism, i.e., using an invigilation application for tests and prevention of cheating such as HONORLOCK.
3. Expanding training to reduce technical errors and technical support requests.
4. Dispatching educational messages for students and faculty members explaining respect of others as a code of conduct during the distance education period.
5. Organizing workshops and courses for faculty members on conducting online assessment, and developing an assessment mechanism to adhere to it.
6. Training in this domain is significant for both the student and the teacher.
7. Using simulation in practicum courses, while giving more weight to oral tests and class discussions.

8. Presenting an orientation lecture for students to clarify rights and duties, and to increase trust between the student and the faculty member.
9. Educating students on the importance of commitment in distance education and its significance in developing their skills.
10. Adopting oral tests in some disciplines that rely on analysis or acting (Role Play).
11. Conducting assessment using question banks and random question feature.

The 8th Meeting: Quality of Education and Research Processes During COVID-19 Crisis and Future Approaches

Highlighting the vital role of academic departments' heads and supervisors to render the educational and research processes a success, and to overcome challenges at this stage, the meeting presented a series of lectures. As the Forum seeks to support all faculty members in the Kingdom, it invited faculty members from all Saudi universities. The Forum, hosting an elite group of presenters, spanned over seven days. The Ministry of Education Undersecretary for University Education, Dr. Abdulrahman Alkhorayf, presented the final lecture on university education efforts during the COVID-19 pandemic crisis and the future approaches. The following are the most important recommendations in the series of lectures that tackled the educational and research processes:

1. All challenges and threats pertaining to online assessment should be put into consideration.
2. The principles of assessment should be emphasized to guarantee justice and equality to all students.
3. Methods of assessing students on practical parts should be considered.
4. Alternatives should be found to assessment methods of the learning outcomes that cannot be applied online.

5. Cooperation for inter-disciplinary research between all University sectors should be encouraged to promote research excellence locally and internationally.
6. Research projects should be encouraged.
7. Research competencies should be built.
8. From a student perspective, challenges to return to campus include education, learning, health, assessment, and transportation; therefore, transparency, honesty, and learning from others are the best way to overcome these challenges.
9. Focusing on students is one of the most important pillars of creative academic leadership.
10. Different Pre COVID-19 education and Post COVID-19 education gives us two main dimensions: educational quality and efficiency of spending.
11. Academic departments are the core for the success of university education, and therefore they need more support, empowerment and flexibility for change and development to keep pace with recent developments and changes.
12. Establishing the Centre of Innovation for Education to stimulate academic departments to work on interactive creative electronic courses.

This case study is an example of how universities and all faculty must work together in times of crisis.

References

Ahmed, A. 2020. Educational Leadership during the coronavirus pandemic. The International Council for Open and Distance Education (ICDE).

Ahmed, S. A. et al. 2020. Model for Utilizing Distance Learning post COVID-19 using (PACT)TM A Cross Sectional Qualitative Study. BMC Medical Education, preprint.

Ahmed, S., Shehata, M. and Hassanien, M. 2020. Emerging Faculty Needs for Enhancing Student Engagement on a Virtual Platform, MedEdPublish.

Aiello, A. 2015. The Effect of Reactive School Closure on Community Influenza-Like Illness Counts in the State of Michigan During the 2009 H1N1 Pandemic. Clinical Infectious Diseases, Volume 60, Issue 12, pp 90–97.

Al-Hanawi, M. K. et al. 2020. Knowledge, Attitude and Practice Toward COVID-19 Among the Public in the Kingdom of Saudi Arabia: A Cross-Sectional Study, Frontiers in Public Health. Frontiers Media S.A., 8, p. 217.

Al-Rabiaah, A., Temsah, M.H., Al-Eyadhy, A.A., Hasan, G.M., Al-Zamil, F., Al-Subaie, S., Alsohime, F., Jamal, A., Alhaboob, A., Al-Saadi, B. and Somily, A.M. 2020. Middle East Respiratory Syndrome-Corona Virus (MERS-CoV) associated stress among medical students at a university teaching hospital in Saudi Arabia. Journal of Infection and Public Health, 13(5), pp.687-691.

Alrefaie, Z., Hassanien, M. and Al-Hayani, A. 2020. Monitoring Online Learning During COVID-19 Pandemic; Suggested Online Learning Portfolio (COVID-19 OLP), MedEdPublish. Association for Medical Education in Europe (AMEE), 9(1).

AI-Youbi, A. O. et al. 2020. The King Abdulaziz University (KAU) Pandemic Framework: A Methodological Approach to Leverage Social Media for the Sustainable Management of Higher Education in Crisis, Sustainability. MDPI AG, 12(11), p. 4367.

Alruwais, N., Wills, G. and Wald, M. 2018. Advantages and challenges of using e-assessment. International Journal of Information and Education Technology, 8(1), pp. 34-37.

Alston, J. 17 March 2020. What impact has the coronavirus had on higher education? INOMICS.

Araújo e Sá, M.H. and Pinto, S. 2020. Introduction: language management, ideologies and practices in scientific research. European Journal of Higher Education, pp. 1-8.

Arend, B. 2007. Course assessment practices and student learning strategies in online courses. Journal of Asynchronous Learning Networks, 11(4), pp. 3-13.

Beckman, T., Lam, H. and Khare, A. 2017. Learning Assessment Must Change in a World of Digital "Cheats". In Phantom Ex Machina pp. 211-222. Springer, Cham.

Beebe, R., Vonderwell, S. and Boboc, M. 2010. Emerging patterns in transferring assessment practices from F2F to online environments. Electronic Journal of e-learning, 8(1), pp.1-12.

Bothwell, E. (2020a). March 18, 2020. Flexible admissions could mitigate Covid-19 impact.

Bothwell, E. (2020b). March 19, 2020. Coronavirus could be 'make or break' for universities' finances.

Bower, M. 1996. The Will to Manage. McGraw-Hill.

Bridges W. 2004. Transitions: Making Sense of Life's Changes. Cambridge, MA: Da Capo Press.

Cameron, E. and Green, M. 2015. Making sense of change management, 4th Ed. London: Kogan Page.

Cheng, R. March 19, 2020. The COVID-19 Crisis and International Students. March 19, 2020.

Cummings, S., Bridgman, T., and Brown, KG. 2016. Unfreezing change as three steps: Rethinking Kurt Lewin's legacy for change management. Human Relations. 69(1):33-60.

Daniel, S.J. 2020. Education and the COVID-19 pandemic. Prospects, pp.1-6.

Dawson, P. and Sutherland-Smith, W. 2017. Can markers detect contract cheating? Results from a pilot study. Assessment and Evaluation in Higher Education, pp.1-8.

de Oliveira Araújo, F.J., de Lima, L.S.A., Cidade, P.I.M., Nobre, C.B. and Neto, M.L.R. 2020. Impact of Sars-Cov- 2 and its reverberation in global higher education and mental health. Psychiatry Research, 288, p. 112977.

Dill, E., Fischer, K., McMurtrie, B., and Supiano, B. 2020. As Coronavirus Spreads, the Decision to Move Classes Online Is the First Step. What Comes Next?

Dodge, R., Daly, A.P., Huyton, J. and Sanders, L.D. 2012. The challenge of defining wellbeing. International Journal of Wellbeing, 2(3).

Donovan, J., Mader, C. and Shinsky, J. 2007. Online vs. traditional course evaluation formats: Student perceptions. Journal of Interactive Online Learning, 6(3), pp.158-180.

Draper, M.J., Ibezim, V. and Newton, P.M. 2017. Are Essay Mills committing fraud? An analysis of their behaviours vs the 2006 Fraud Act (UK). International Journal for Educational Integrity, 13(1), p.3.

Eljinini, M.A.H., Alsamarai, S., Hameed, S. and Amawi, A. 2012. The Impact of E-assessments system on the success of the implementation process. International Journal of Modern Education and Computer Science, 4(11), p.76.

Ellaway, R. and Masters, K. 2008. AMEE Guide 32: e-Learning in medical education Part 1: Learning, teaching and assessment. Medical teacher, 30(5), pp. 455-473.

Frieden, T. March 11, 2020. Lessons from Ebola: The secret of successful epidemic response. CNN.

Garcia, F. 2006. Effective leadership response to crisis. Strategy & Leadership, 34(1), pp. 4–10.

Gardner, J. 2017. Leading projects. In: Swanwick, T., McKimm, J. (Editors). ABC of Clinical Leadership, 2nd Ed. Chichester: John Wiley & Sons; pp. 43-49.

Gaytan, J., and McEwen, B. C. 2007. Effective online instructional and assessment strategies. The American Journal of Distance Education, 21(3), pp. 117-132.

Gilbert, L., Whitelock, D. and Gale, V. 2011. Synthesis report on assessment and feedback with technology enhancement. University of Southampton, UK: Electronics and Computer Science EPrints.

Glendinning, I. 2017. Scorecard for Academic Integrity Development: Benchmarks and evaluation of institutional strategies. Conference proceedings for Plagiarism Across Europe and Beyond, Brno, Czech Republic, pp. 25-34.

Goleman, D. 1995. Emotional Intelligence. New York: Bantam Books.

Guo, Y.R., Cao, Q.D., Hong, Z.S., Tan, Y.Y., Chen, S.D., Jin, H.J., Tan, K.S., Wang, D.Y. and Yan, Y. 2020. The origin, transmission and clinical therapies on coronavirus disease 2019 (COVID-19) outbreak–an update on the status. Military Medical Research, 7(1), pp.1-10.

Hannafin, M., Oliver, K., Hill, J. R., Glazer, E., and Sharma, P. 2003. Cognitive and learning factors in web-based distance learning environments. In M. G. Moore & W. G. Anderson (Eds.), Handbook of Distance Education, pp. 245-260. Mahwah, NJ: Erlbaum.

Harvard University. Coronavirus (COVID-19). 2020.

Hashem, A. M. et al. 2020. Therapeutic use of chloroquine and hydroxychloroquine in COVID-19 and other viral infections: A narrative review, Travel Medicine and Infectious Disease. Elsevier USA.

Heifetz, R.A., Heifetz, R., Grashow, A. and Linsky, M. 2009. The practice of adaptive leadership: Tools and tactics for changing your organization and the world. Harvard Business Press.

Heifetz, RA., Grashow, A., Linsky, M. 2009. Leadership in a (permanent) crisis. Harvard Business Review, 62(9), p.153.

Herrmann, N., and Herrmann-Nehdi, A. 2015. The Whole Brain business book: Unlocking the power of whole brain thinking in organizations, teams, and individuals. McGraw Hill Professional.

Hines, RN. 2020. SOT 59th annual meeting canceled.

Hope, J. 2020. Be aware of how COVID-19 could impact international students. The Successful Registrar, 20, pp. 1-8.

Horbach, S. 2020. Pandemic Publishing: Medical journals drastically speed up their publication process for Covid-19. bioRxiv.

Hu, Y., Sun, J., Dai, Z., Deng, H., Li, X., Huang, Q., Wu, Y., Sun, L. and Xu, Y. 2020. Prevalence and severity of corona virus disease 2019 (COVID-19): A systematic review and meta-analysis. Journal of Clinical Virology, p.104371.

Illanes, P., Law, J., Mendy, A., Sanghvi, S., Sarakatsannis, J. March 2020. Coronavirus and the campus: How can US higher education organize to respond? University World News.

Inceoglu, I. and Warr, P. 2011. Personality and job engagement. Journal of Personnel Psychology.

INOMICS Team. 2015. Supervision - tips for PhDs supervising bachelor's or master's students for the first time.

JISC. 2016. Project management.

Kang, L., Li, Y., Hu, S., Chen, M., Yang, C., Yang, B.X., Wang, Y., Hu, J., Lai, J., Ma, X. and Chen, J. 2020. The mental health of medical workers in Wuhan, China dealing with the 2019 novel coronavirus. The Lancet Psychiatry, 7(3), p.e14.

Kanter, R.M. April 30, 2020. Leading Your Team Past the Peak of a Crisis. Harvard Business Review (website).

Kelly, Éanna. July 9, 2020. Universities prepare for the new post-pandemic world. Business Insider.

Kernick, D., Swanwick, T. 2017. Leading in complex environments. In: Swanwick, T., McKimm, J., Editors. ABC of Clinical Leadership. 2nd Ed. Chichester: John Wiley & Sons.

Kim, H.J. and Cameron, G.T. 2011. Emotions matter in crisis: The role of anger and sadness in the public's response to crisis news framing and corporate crisis response. Communication Research, 38(6), pp. 826-855.

Kim, N., Smith, M.J., and Maeng, K. 2008. Assessment in online distance education: A comparison of three online programs at a university. Online Journal of Distance Learning Administration, 11(1).

Kingston University London. 2 April 2020. Coronavirus Covid-19 – latest update on Kingston University's response.

Kotter, J.P. 1996. Leading change. Brighton (MA): Harvard Business Press.

Kotter, J.P. and Schlesinger, L.A. 1989. Choosing strategies for change. In: Asch, D., Bowman, C., Eds. Readings in Strategic Management. London: Palgrave Macmillan, p. 294-306.

Kralik, D., Visentin, K., van Loon, A. 2006. Transition: a literature review. Journal of Advanced Nursing, 55(3), pp. 320–329.

Kübler-Ross, E. and Kessler, D. 2009. The five stages of grief. In Library of Congress Catalog in in Publication Data Ed., On Grief and Grieving, pp. 7-30.

Lancaster, T. and Draper, M. April 2020. Assessing with Integrity. QAA workshops.

Lauka, J.D., McCarthy, A.K. and Carter, D.A. 2014. A national survey on counseling training clinics in CACREP-accredited programs. Journal of Counseling in Illinois, 3(1), pp.5-16.

Lee, K. March 10, 2020. Coronavirus: universities are shifting classes online – but it's not as easy as it sounds.

Lent, J. and Schwartz, R. 2012. The impact of work setting, demographic characteristics, and personality factors related to burnout among professional counselors. Journal of Mental Health Counseling, 34(4), pp.355-372.

Lewin, K. 1951. In: Cartwright D, Ed. Field Theory in Social Science: Selected Theoretical Papers. New York: Harper & Brothers.

Lewin, K. 2016. Frontiers in group dynamics: Concept, method and reality in social science; social equilibria and social change. Human relations.

Lim, M. 2020. Educating despite the COVID-19 outbreak: lessons from Singapore.

Llamas-Nistal, M., Fernández-Iglesias, M.J., González-Tato, J. and Mikic-Fonte, F.A. 2013. Blended e-assessment: Migrating classical exams to the digital world. Computers & Education, 62, pp.72-87.

Ma, H. and Miller, C. 2020. Trapped in a Double Bind: Chinese Overseas Student Anxiety during the COVID-19 Pandemic. Health Communication, pp.1-8.

Magallanes, M. 2020. Letter to Taylor Students During COVID-19.

Maican, C.I., Cazan, A.M., Lixandroiu, R.C. and Dovleac, L. 2019. A study on academic staff personality and technology acceptance: The case of communication and collaboration applications. Computers & Education, 128, pp. 113-131.

Malloy, J. 2020. Stop making graduate students pay up front for conferences. Nature, 13.

Marriott, P. 2009. Students' evaluation of the use of online summative assessment on an undergraduate financial accounting module. British Journal Educational Technology, 40(2), pp. 237–254.

Maslow, A.H. 1981. Motivation and personality. Prabhat Prakashan.

McKimm, J. 2008. COINNS: A new framework for personal, professional and educational developers. Presentation at ASME conference, September 2008, Leicester.

McKimm, J. 2009. Professional development for medical educators and clinical teachers: challenges and opportunities. South East Asian Journal of Medical Education, 3(2), pp.3-8.

McKimm, J. and Jones, P.K. 2018. Twelve tips for applying change models to curriculum design, development and delivery. Medical Teacher, 40(5), pp.520-526.

McKimm, J. and O'Sullivan, H. 2016. When I say… leadership. Medical Education, 9(50), pp.896-897.

McKimm, J., Gibbs, T., Bishop, J. and Jones, P.K. 2020. Health Professions' Educators' Adaptation to Rapidly Changing Circumstances: The Ottawa 2020 Conference Experience. Med Ed Publish, 9.

McKinsey & Company. March 2020. Leadership in a crisis: Responding to the coronavirus outbreak and future challenges.

Meyerowitz-Katz, G. and Merone, L. 2020. A systematic review and meta-analysis of published research data on COVID-19 infection-fatality rates. medRxiv.

Mintzberg H.A. and Lampel B.J. 1998. Strategy Safari: A guided tour through the wilds of strategic management. Wiltshire: The Free Press.

Mintzberg, H. 1987. The strategy concept I: Five Ps for strategy. California management review, 30(1), pp.11-24.

Mitchell, T., Aldridge, N., Williamson, W.M. and Broomhead, P. 2003. Computer-based testing of medical knowledge. In Proceedings of the 7th computer assisted assessment conference (pp. 249–267). Loughborough.

Moir, F., Yielder, J., Sanson, J. and Chen, Y. 2018. Depression in medical students: current insights. Advances in medical education and practice, 9, p.323.

Mostrous, A. and Kenber, B. January 2016. Universities face student cheating crisis. The Times.

Muilenburg, L. Y. and Berge, Z. L. 2005. Student barriers to online learning: A factor analytic study. Distance Education, 26(1), pp. 29-48.

Naismith, L., Lee, B.H. and Pilkington, R.M. 2011. Collaborative learning with a wiki: Differences in perceived usefulness in two contexts of use. Journal of Computer Assisted Learning, 27(3), 228242.

Nassisi, M., Audo, I., Zeitz, C., Varin, J., Wohlschlegel, J., Smirnov, V., Santiard-Baron, D., Picaud, S. and Sahel, J.A. 2020. Impact of the COVID-19 lockdown on basic science research in ophthalmology: the experience of a highly specialized research facility in France. Eye, pp.1-2.

Newton, P. 2015. Academic integrity: A quantitative study of confidence and understanding in students at the start of their higher education. Assessment and Evaluation in Higher Education, 41(3), pp. 482-497.

Omary, M.B., Eswaraka, J., Kimball, S.D., Moghe, P.V., Panettieri Jr., R.A. and Scotto, K.W. 2020. The COVID-19 pandemic and research shutdown: staying safe and productive. J Clin Invest, 130(6), pp. 2745–2748.

Oncu, S. and Cakir, H. 2011. Research in online learning environments: Priorities and methodologies. Computers & Education, 57(1), pp. 1098-1108.

Peters Thomas, J. and Waterman Robert, H. 1982. In search of excellence: lessons from America's best-run companies. NY: Harper & Row, Publishers Inc.

Raaheim, A., Mathiassen, K., Moen, V., Lona, I., Gynnild, V., Bunæs, B.R. and Hasle, E.T. 2019. Digital assessment–how does it challenge local practices and national law? A Norwegian case study. European Journal of Higher Education, 9(2), pp.219-231.

Randall, L.M. and Coakley, L.A. 2007. Applying adaptive leadership to successful change initiatives in academia. Leadership & Organization Development Journal.

Rath, T., Harter, J.K. and Harter, J. 2010. Wellbeing: The five essential elements. Simon and Schuster.

Reimers, F and Schleicher, A. 2020. Development: A framework to guide an education response to the COVID-19 Pandemic of 2020. OCED.

Ridgway, J., McCusker, S. and Pead, D. 2004. Literature review of e-assessment.

Robbins, A. 2014. The 6 Human Needs: Why We Do What We Do.

Robins, R. March 16, 2020. STAT's guide to health care conferences disrupted by the coronavirus crisis.

Rogers, E.M. 2003. Diffusion of innovations. 5th Ed. New York: Free Press.

Ross, J. March 16, 2020. Coronavirus hit to Australian students' finances.

Rossi, P.G., Broccoli, S., Angelini, P. and Emilia-Romagna COVID-19 working group. 2020. Case fatality rate in patients with COVID-19 infection and its relationship with length of follow up. Journal of Clinical Virology.

Roubein, R., Ehley, B. and Goldberg, D. 2020. Coronavirus threat gives strapped state health agencies a new crisis.

Salcedo, A., Yar, S. and Cherelus, G. May 8, 2020. Coronavirus Travel Restrictions, Across the Globe.

Saraswat, R., Saraswat, D.A. 2020. Research opportunities in pandemic lockdown. Science, 368(6491), pp. 594-595.

Schwartzstein, R.M., Huang G.C. and Coughlin, C.M. 2008. Development and implementation of a comprehensive strategic plan for medical education at an academic medical center. Academic Medicine, 83(6), pp. 550-559.

Service, R. 2020. 'The disruption is enormous.' Coronavirus epidemic snarls science worldwide. Science(17).

Shaffer, K.S., Love, M.M., Chapman, K.M., Horn, A.J., Haak, P.P. and Shen, C.Y. 2017. Walk-in triage systems in university counseling centers. Journal of College Student Psychotherapy, 31(1), pp. 71-89.

Simonson, M., Smaldino, S. E., Albright, M. and Zvacek, S. 2006. Teaching and learning at a distance: Foundations of distance education (3rd Ed.). Upper Saddle River, NJ: Merrill/Prentice Hall.

Sorensen, E. 2013. Implementation and student perceptions of e-assessment in a Chemical Engineering module. European Journal of Engineering Education, 38(2), pp. 172-185.

Spurlock, D. 2020. Scholarship During a Pandemic: Secondary Data Analysis. Journal of Nursing Education. 59(5):245-247.

Stacey, RD. 2001. Complex Responsive Processes in Organisations. London: Routledge.

Swan, K. 2001. Virtual interaction: Design factors affecting student satisfaction and perceived learning in asynchronous online courses. Distance Education, 22(2), pp. 306-331.

Thompson, G. 2020. Reflecting on relational needs in the context of a global health crisis.

Thornton, L.F. 2013. 7 Lenses: Learning the Principles and Practices of Ethical Leadership. Richmond VA: Leading in Context LLC.

Timmis, S., Broadfoot, P., Sutherland, R. and Oldfield, A. 2016. Rethinking assessment in a digital age: Opportunities, challenges and risks. British Educational Research Journal, 42(3), pp. 454-476.

Tubaishat, A., Bhatti, A. and El-Qawasmeh, E. 2006. ICT experiences in two different Middle Eastern universities. Issues in informing science & information technology, 3.

UNESCO. 2020a. Half of world's student population not attending school: UNESCO launches global coalition to accelerate deployment of remote learning solutions.

UNESCO. 2020b. Adverse consequences of school closure.

UNESCO. 2020c. COVID-19 Educational Disruption and Response.

UNESCO. 2020d. 90 million students out of school due to COVID-19: UNESCO releases first global numbers and mobilizes response.

UNESCO. 2020e. COVID-19: 10 Recommendations to plan distance learning solutions.

UNESCO. 2020f. Education Response to COVID-19 in the Caribbean SIDS.

Van Bavel, J.J., Baicker, K., Boggio, P.S., Capraro, V., Cichocka, A., Cikara, M., Crockett, M.J., Crum, A.J., Douglas, K.M., Druckman, J.N. and Drury, J. 2020. Using social and behavioural science to support COVID-19 pandemic response. Nature Human Behaviour, pp.1-12.

Vogan, C.L., McKimm, J., Da Silva, A.L. and Grant, A. 2014. Twelve tips for providing effective student support in undergraduate medical education. Medical teacher, 36(6), pp. 480-485.

Weissgerber, T., Bediako, Y., De Winde, C.M., Ebrahimi, H., Fernández-Chiappe, F., Ilangovan, V., Mehta, D., Quezada, C.P., Riley, J.L., Saladi, S.M. and Sarabipour, S. 2020. Point of View: Mitigating the impact of conference and travel cancellations on researchers' futures. Elife, 9, 57032.

Way, A. 2012. The use of e-assessments in the Nigerian higher education system. Turkish Online J. Distance Education, vol. 13, no. 1, pp. 140–152.

Whalen B. 2020. Education Abroad in a Post-COVID-19 World.

Whitelock, D., Ruedel, C. and Mackenzie, D., 2006. e-Assessment case studies of effective and innovative practice. Final report for JISC ITT funded project conducted by The Open University (Milton Keynes) and University of Derby.

Williams, J.B. and Wong, A. 2009. The efficacy of final examinations: A comparative study of closed-book, invigilated exams and open-book, open-web exams. British Journal of Educational Technology, 40(2), pp. 227-236.

Wu, F., Zhao, S., Yu, B., Chen, Y.M., Wang, W., Song, Z.G., Hu, Y., Tao, Z.W., Tian, J.H., Pei, Y.Y. and Yuan, M.L. 2020. A new coronavirus associated with human respiratory disease in China. Nature, 579(7798), pp. 265-269.

Xiang, Y.T., Yang, Y., Li, W., Zhang, L., Zhang, Q., Cheung, T. and Ng, C.H. 2020. Timely mental health care for the 2019 novel coronavirus outbreak is urgently needed. The Lancet Psychiatry, 7(3), pp. 228-229.

Zhang, L., Shen, F.M., Chen, F. and Lin, Z. 2020. Origin and evolution of the 2019 novel coronavirus. Clinical Infectious Diseases.

Zhu, X. and Liu, J. 2020. Education in and After Covid-19: Immediate Responses and Long-Term Visions. Postdigital Science and Education, pp. 1-5.